GOOD TIMES ... BAD TIMES

by

John Parsons

Best Wishes.

John Parsons.

'GOOD TIMES – BAD TIMES'

Published in 2005 by **Beanshoots**

First Edition, 2005, printed for the Education Authorities with the permission of the author, John Parsons, and not for sale to the general public.

Second Edition, 2005, edited and published by Beanshoots. Printed and bound by Wessex Malthouse Direct, Taunton.

The right of John Parsons to be identified as the author of this book has been asserted by him in accordance with the Copyright, Designs and Patents Act 1988.

Published by **Beanshoots**
Deer Holt, Ellicombe, TA24 6TT
01643 703597

ISBN 0-9551693-0-5

Cover photograph of road bridge at Bishops Lydeard Station © **Beanshoots**

A fictional tale of a railwayman and his family, based on information obtained from entries made in a log book, by three Stationmasters at Bishops Lydeard Station, Somerset, during the period from 1870 – 1926.

CONTENTS

PREFACE

On the West Somerset Railway we hold classes for school children in the area on a range of subjects, and a short while ago I gave a talk entitled, 'A Drover's Tale', which was a 'factional tale' of a porter at Bishops Lydeard station during the Victorian era. This formed part of a history lesson, on Victorian England, for the National Curriculum Stage 2.

Later I was offered on loan, for research purposes, a preserved copy of the original Stationmaster's logbook for Bishops Lydeard station for the period from the 1880s to the 1920s and was asked if there was any way that I could reproduce the material in this log, so that it could be read by a larger audience.

Because the period covered by the log book overlapped a large part of the period covered by the talk I felt that both subjects could be enhanced by being combined.

I have, therefore, turned the talk into the written word, and after a number of minor amendments to coincide with the details shown in the log, have incorporated both texts into one volume. All the passages which I have reproduced verbatim from the log are in *italics*, while passages reproduced from my original talk are in the standard print format.

CHILDHOOD MEMORIES

Grandpa Hawkes and his sons had eked out a living on the hill farms around Exmoor for many years. Times were hard; my father could not find any work on Exmoor so he trudged from farm to farm seeking work, until he came to the village of Combe Florey in the county of Somerset. Here he was lucky and obtained a labourer's job on a local farm, with a tied cottage, which went with the job. He then sent for my Mother to join him and she arrived in the village, on the local carrier's cart in 1845.

I was born in 1848 in the eleventh year of the reign of our Queen Victoria, and my parents christened me Cuthbert, a name I disliked, but fortunately, everyone I knew called me Jon.

Eventually my parents had another two sons, and a daughter, which meant there were six of us living in a two-bedroomed cottage. I do not know how they managed it, but they sent us all to the local penny school and we managed to learn to read and write and to do our sums. I stayed at school until I was twelve years old, but my youngest brother and my sister were not so fortunate and had to leave school, and go into 'service' to help with the family income, and ease the overcrowding in our small cottage. Whilst we were at school we often had to take time off in the summer months, to help the rest of the families in the village with the harvest.

When I was about to leave school, people started to talk about the 'Railway' that was going to come; at first we did not believe these stories because nothing seemed to be happening. Then, suddenly, a lot of men who people called 'navvies' and who spoke in a strange way, started to set up camps in the area, and then slowly a long scar appeared across the countryside, following the course that the railway was to take. Cutting through hills and dividing farms into two parts, for a time it was impossible for some families to visit each other, even though they only lived a short distance away, without making a long detour, because of the earthworks.

The navvies who came to build the railway were tough men, many of whom had worked on building other railway lines around the country. Often their wives travelled with them from camp to camp.

Very often the odd sheep would vanish from a farmer's flock and the navvies always got the blame. Then the local constable would be called, but he never managed to catch the culprit, because by the time the constable arrived all the evidence had vanished. Often people's sleep would be shattered at weekends when it came to closing time in the local hostelries. The local policeman managed to arrest some of the culprits, usually when they were too drunk to stand up, and although sometimes the local lads were just as guilty as the navvies, it always seemed that it was the navvies that finished up spending a night in the cells. They were brought before the local magistrate on the following Monday morning, and were then fined 1/- (5p). This seemed to make little difference; they were often back in the cells the following weekend.

After the line opened and the navvies departed to find work in other areas, peace and tranquillity returned to the district. A few people who had been employed on building the railway, and who had got to know some of the local lassies, decided to stay around. When the railway opened some of them managed to get jobs as 'gangers' or 'lengthsmen' and it was their job to ensure that the track on which the trains ran was kept in good condition. As there was a shortage of jobs in the district, there was a lot of resentment that these strangers were getting work, when many people living in the area were unemployed, and some local people even finished up in the 'Poor House'. But as they had built the railway, they knew what to look for and what to do if anything did go wrong, and it also meant that the railway did not have pay to train more staff, which meant the company was happy.

We could not see that the coming of the railway was likely to affect our lives and many thought it would be a lot of nonsense.

The railway had not been opened when I had to leave school and find work.

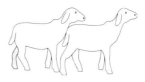

A WORKING LAD

After I left school there was no work available on any of the farms around the village. But eventually I managed to get a job working as a Drover's lad, helping the Drover to get the sheep or cattle to market. It was our job to try to ensure that, if possible, we did not lose any animals on the way to market, that they were rested regularly, and properly fed in order to try to get the best prices for them. Sometimes we were tempted to try to get them to market earlier, so that we would be back home sooner; but we knew that if we attempted to do this the animals would lose more weight, and if he did not get the best price in the market, we would be in trouble with the farmer when we returned home.

When we had walked all the way to market with the beasts, we then had to walk all the way back home and, if the markets were in London or in the Midlands, we could be away for up to a month. We met lots of people on the way to the various markets, who looked after me because at first I was rather skinny. Eventually, because of all the exercise and good food, I grew to a height of six foot and was strong enough to carry bales of straw or a sheep under each arm.

In the Spring and Summer months we usually took the cattle, sheep, or sometimes geese to market along the 'Drover's Roads'. These roads, like the Ridgeway in Wiltshire, ran across the top of the Downs, and because the drainage was better, the ground was firmer even if there had been some rain. Of course it was also a little cooler up on the

Downs during the hot Summer months and this, together with the firmer ground, meant that the going was much easier for the animals, and they did not tire so easily. The only problem was that these routes avoided many of the villages, and so we often had to take it in turns to sleep under the stars. We could not all go to sleep at the same time in case the animals wandered off, or the sheep were attacked by foxes. The farmers, to whom the animals belonged, did not mind us going this way because we avoided using the Toll roads which were expensive.

When we were up on the Downs walking along the Ridgeway we began to realise what an impact the railway was starting to have on other parts of the country. Sometimes we stopped on the top of the Downs near the village of Swindon and could see the large factory that had been erected to manufacture and service engines for the railway. Every time we passed that way they seemed to be building another extension to the factory, and they had also built a new village to house all the people they needed to work there.

In the Autumn and Winter it was different. It was much colder and windier on the Downs, and we could not run the risk of being stranded up there if it should start to snow, and of losing animals in snow drifts. Although the conditions were often very unpleasant for us we could always make up a fire to sit or sleep around at night, but the animals did not have even have this small luxury, and no matter how carefully we looked after them, we nearly always lost a few on the way to market in the Winter.

It was hard work, and although I sometimes grumbled when I was thoroughly cold or soaking wet, or both, I did enjoy the work, but not when I had to sleep in the open under a hedge in the pouring rain or in the snow in the middle of Winter. Had I known how little time I had before I would be once again be walking around the local area trying to find work, or how long before I would be able to get any work, other than casual labouring, perhaps I would have been more grateful for the job I had.

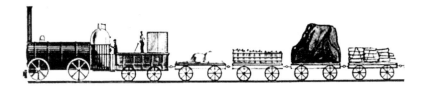

UNEMPLOYED

When the railway first arrived, everyone assumed the main source of income for the line would be passengers, and so at first the station only had the small building required to house the booking office, and entrance hall, the waiting room, and the Ladies and Gents toilets, together with a short platform for the passengers to board the train.

After the branch line had been open for a while it was realised that the passenger traffic was insufficient for the line to prosper. Many people said that Mr Gould, who was the first Stationmaster at Bishops Lydeard, managed to obtain more business for the Great Western Railway in the public bars of the Farmer's Arms or the Lethbridge Arms than he ever did in his office at the railway station. In those establishments he started to talk to the local farmers and suggested to them that, "If you let me know when you want to send your next lot of animals to market, I will arrange to have all the wagons you need at the station to send them away, and what is more they will be in London the next day, rested, and the railway will feed and water them on their journey."

He also went round to visit those few farmers he had not met in the pubs, and leaning on their farm gates told them the same story. Now the farmers in the area were, like farmers everywhere, reluctant to change their ways in a hurry. Eventually one of the locals was persuaded to send his cows to London by train.

When the day came that the livestock were due to be sent, the wagons that the animals were to travel in arrived on time, all cleaned out, and with fresh straw in each wagon. Although the train arrived on time the farmer did not. Eventually he arrived with his livestock an hour late. Although the unfortunate beasts were loaded into the wagons as quickly as possible, because the branch line was a single track, with the exception of the passing loop at Williton, no other trains could pass, either up or down the line, until the cattle train been loaded and had departed.

Nor were the unfortunate Mr Gould's problems finished after the train had left. Apart from reports that had to be sent to the District Manager to explain why both passenger and goods trains had been delayed, the only method of loading the cattle into the wagons was by using the passenger platform. The shouting of the porters trying to get the beasts on the train in a hurry, the unaccustomed hissing noises from the waiting engine, together with the unknown environment that the poor animals found themselves in was rather too much. In spite of all the efforts of the staff to clean the platform before the next passenger train arrived, they were not entirely successful, and Mr Gould was then besieged by a number of extremely annoyed ladies who found that the hems of their (long) dresses had become rather soiled on the mucky platform.

In spite of the problems, the farmer who had taken the plunge was pleased with the fact that his cattle had arrived in the capital the following day, and he had been paid promptly.

That story was told to me one night, by my friend Bill Bond when we were having a quick half of cider in the Farmer's Arms. I had known Bill since we were at school, and he was employed at Bishops Lydeard Station as a porter. He was laughing so much as he told me the story that I thought he would never remember that it was his turn to buy the next round!

He also went on to tell me that the managers in the District Civil Engineers office at Bristol had decided that if more traffic of this type was to be accepted by the railway then obviously the arrangements would have to be improved. After several meetings on the site it was decided that a short length of track, (he called it a siding) should run from, and parallel to, the running line and adjacent to the siding they would build a cattle pen, to load the livestock onto the wagons. Also a goods shed would be built, so that the rapidly increasing amount of general goods that were being handled at the station, could be loaded on and off the railway wagons, and to and from the road vehicles. This could be done under cover, without the work being delayed due to bad weather, nor would other trains be delayed whilst the wagons were being loaded or unloaded. They also decided that an area on the opposite side of the track to the station buildings should be cleared, an approach road built, and sidings laid so that coal and timber traffic could be handled at the station.

When this work was finished, all the farmers had to do was to arrange to deliver the animals to the station, for them to be shipped to many large towns, in the Midlands or to London. This, of course, was too good an offer for the local farmers to refuse, and so before long my work mate and I were without a job, and facing the risk of finishing up in the local workhouse. As an experienced Drover, my mate was lucky; he managed to get work as a shepherd and with the job a tied cottage for his wife and children to live in.

I learned that work had started on extending the railway line from Watchet to Minehead, and I walked to Washford one day to see if there was any chance of work on the new railway, but work had been underway for 18 months. Navvies had come from all over the country to do the work, and once they had started they seldom left the site unless they were killed or injured, or they wanted to go to the local ale house. Perhaps it was just as well that I did not get a job there, because I heard that sometimes they did not get paid when they should have been, and on one occasion the frightened Clerk of the Works had to keep the irate navvies at bay with a loaded pistol, until the local militia arrived to read the Riot Act.

There were not many other jobs about but I managed to get by for almost two years with casual farm labouring jobs, including lambing, sheep shearing, sowing and lifting potatoes and helping with the harvest in the summer. As I had nowhere else to stay I went back to live with my parents. Conditions were still crowded, but the extra money that I brought into the house was a help, even though it was only a very small amount.

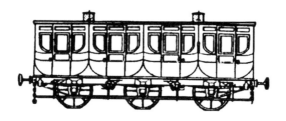

WORKING ON THE RAILWAY

In July 1874 my friend Bob informed me that Cyril Waltham had been made up (promoted) to a charge hand, and would be moving to Minehead station. This meant there would be a vacancy at Bishops Lydeard station for a porter.

He also told me that Mr Gould had been moved to the new station at Blue Anchor. Was it just a coincidence, I often wondered afterwards, that as far as I was aware, they never handled any livestock there? He said that if I was interested in the porter's job, I should get over to the station as soon as possible, because the new Stationmaster Mr A.J. Elliott had already arrived. I went down to the Station the following morning, and Mr Elliott, who was a newcomer to the area, was rather surprised how quickly news managed to get around. I had a long wait in the Waiting Room, whilst a number of members of staff trooped in and out of the stationmaster's office, which was shared with the booking office. Often they came out looking rather more glum than when they went in.

Mr Elliott was a rather short man, only about 5 feet 6 inches tall, slim, with a weather-beaten face, and a rather resplendent waxed moustache. He was young, about 30 years old and ambitious: he had already been promoted three times, and I gathered he had just discovered that things had not been run the way he wanted, when Mr Gould had been in charge.

Furthermore, everybody was left in no doubt that things were going to change from then on.

Just as I was beginning to think that perhaps it was not such a good idea to try for a job on the railway, I was summoned into Mr Elliott's office. His bad mood seemed to have vanished suddenly, and he was very pleasant to me. I was surprised to find myself thinking that in spite of my first impressions, I would enjoy working for him, if I was lucky enough to get the job. He seemed impressed with my standard of writing, and that I could also read and add up. I thought that I was doing rather well until he suddenly asked me why I wanted to work on the railway. I had to think quickly; I could hardly say it was because I'd heard that if you got a job on the railway you had a job for life! After a slight pause, I said that I felt that if I worked hard I would be able to better myself. This answer seemed to impress him, because he did not ask me any further questions, but sat there deep in thought, staring at me for what seemed like ages.

Finally he informed me that I had a job as a porter at the station provided I passed a medical examination, but this appointment would be subject to a month's trial. As Mr Waltham was not moving to Minehead for a fortnight, if I was to prepared to do some simple clerical work for a week, I could start next Monday. I was a bit worried whether I would be able to do the work, but he assured me that I should not have any problems.

When I came out of the office I found that a special train had arrived at the station, and all the staff were loading Mr Gould's household chattels from the stationmaster's house on to the train for removal to Blue Anchor. Later, I learnt that Mr Elliott's belongings also arrived by special train. Shortly after this, household removals by rail became rather popular. Sometimes on Quarter Days tenant farmers would give up their tenancy, moving to another (often larger) farm. Provided they were given sufficient notice, the railway would then send a special train to collect all his livestock, farm equipment including carts, feeders, bailers, ploughs etc., and his family and household goods, then transport them to their new farm which was often some distance away. This business eventually became an important source of revenue to the railway.

After my interview I could not get home fast enough to tell my parents the good news. They were amazed when I told them that I would be earning more in a week than I had ever earned before £1 9s 6d (£1.47 per week).

Although I arrived early at the station on the next Monday morning, the Company Doctor was already there, and he proceeded to give me a very thorough medical, which seemed to take ages. Finally, he informed Mr Elliott that I had passed the Medical and he could employ me as a lad porter, (the WSR had some rather elderly lad porters in those days), subject of course to the aforementioned four weeks' trial period.

The next shock came when one of my new colleagues started running a tape measure over me and calling out various figures to Mr Elliott, who entered these details onto a rather official looking form. Suddenly the penny dropped, and I realised that they were measuring me for my uniform. I was told that this had to be done in a hurry because the stores van, attached to the branch train which called once a fortnight, was due that morning.

I was then told to get my breakfast, but because I was so nervous I could only manage a cup of tea. After a while Mr Elliott re-appeared having had what seemed to be a rather substantial breakfast. I was given details of the special work I had been brought in to do.

Mr Elliott had decided that if his station was to be run efficiently, a log book was to be created, in which all the information relating to the station was to be recorded. It was my task to start this work under his supervision, using my very best handwriting. Like everything on the railway, there was a suggested format that should be followed, and this was set in front of me, and I was told to copy it into the new book. It read:

Memorandum

This book must be kept by the Officer in charge of the Station and be carefully preserved. It must contain in full the duties allotted to each member of the staff (except Guards and Breaksmen) (sic) paid through the Traffic paybill a copy of which prepared in a tabulated form must be exhibited in the Porters' Room, or other conspicuous place so each man may have his specific duties at hand, and may know what duties are allotted to him. On the list exhibited the name as well as the man's number must be shewn, and as the details recorded thereon are considered standard duties they must not be altered until particulars are submitted to this Office and authority given for the alteration. When a new man is put on or change made in the existing staff the new man will take the duties allotted to the man who caused the change.
This book must contain every special arrangement, or regulation for the working of this Station, which do not

*apply to all Stations alike and are not to be found in the
Book of Rules nor any standard regulation and any
arrangement of a special and exceptional character such
as special privileges or rights possessed by the Public,
special instructions for invoicing or working goods or
other traffic.*

I thought my writing duties had finished when I had
completed this sheet, but Mr Elliott, who, when he had not
been issuing tickets or answering questions from the public,
had been scribbling away on the other desk, passed me a
second sheet to be entered into the log book. When I saw how
many pages were to be written up I began to wonder if I would
ever complete the book before I retired, rather than in one
week. The second sheet read:

Contents

I had not done very much writing since I had left school, so by the time I was halfway through this sheet my arm, wrist and head were aching with all the concentration and effort I was making to avoid mistakes. Fortunately, at this moment there was the sound of raised voices outside on the platform.

Mr Elliott dashed out to see what the problem was, and after two minutes or so, brought in an extremely irate customer. As they entered the office I was told to go to the porters' room in the goods shed and get myself a cup of tea. I needed no second bidding, and the short rest, a cup of tea, and a few minutes in the fresh air meant that I was feeling much better when I was called back into the office.

Mr Elliott explained that the gentleman was rather upset because he had purchased an item from a store, with instructions for it to be despatched in time to ensure it arrived at our station that morning, because it was intended to be a surprise present for his wife.

As I finished the contents list Mr Elliot returned to the office and announced the parcel had arrived. It was a rather heavy object, (we later found out it was a sewing machine complete with stand) packed in a wooden crate. He said he had promised the customer, that as soon as it arrived at the station, he would arrange for someone to deliver it to the customer's house. That someone was to be me, there being no one else available.

Mr Elliott wrote out a note for me to hand to the customer, explaining that the railway was not to blame for the delay, as the store failed to deliver the crate to the forwarding station until the train specified had departed. Bob and I struggled to get the crate onto the 'sack truck' (a two-wheeled type of barrow for moving heavy items). Having collected the note, I set off with the parcel for the customer's house, which everybody had forgotten to mention was at the far end of the village. Having delivered the crate and the letter, I helped the man get it into this house, and received a penny tip for my efforts. At this time I was not sure what the procedure was with tips, but I soon found out that they were an important supplement to our wages, and learnt to pocket them quickly with a polite, "Thank you sir / madam," however small the tip might be. When I finally got back to the station, and put the sack truck away in the goods shed, there was no time to do any further book work and so I signed off and trudged wearily home.

When I opened the book the following morning I found that, whilst I was away from the station, Mr Elliott had made a further two entries in the log. They were:

Identification for Unemployment Insurance purpose
Names of staff employed
A. J. Elliott, Stationmaster
A Pillar, Porter *
C. W. Waltham, Porter +
W. O. Bond, Lad Porter

O. M. Borth, Lad Porter
C. Hawkes, Lad Porter **
* Later made up to Signalman
\+ Made up and transferred to Minehead a fortnight later
** Later made up to Porter and then Signalman / Porter

As my name was on this list it looked as if I might be here to stay.

He had also made the following entry:-

Remittance of cash

The daily cash account at this Station must include all cash received up to and including the receipts of the 7.15pm, and must be remitted to the Bristol cashier by the 8.10am train daily. All receipt books to be produced daily irrespective of whether cash has been collected or not.

Whilst I was glad in one way that he had made some of the entries, because it meant less work for me, I had already realised why I had been given this job. Although Mr Elliott's writing was neat I felt it was not as good as mine, and I was upset that someone else had written in what I had come to regard as 'my book'.

The next document Mr Elliott wanted written in the book without delay, presumably in case his promotion came quicker than he expected, was this:

Stationmaster's certificate on removal from one Station to another

I hereby certify that the whole of the outstanding account, and instructions relating to the working of the Station have been fully explained by me in detail: that the register of stock and non-consumable stores have been checked and the articles handed over; that the duties of the staff and each special instruction in force for the safe proper and convenient working of the Station have been explained verbally, and particulars in writing handed over to Mr .... my successor on his taking charge of the Station.

The petty cash allowance for this Station is £ ..... and I have handed it (or cash vouchers to the amount) to my successor.

Signature of outgoing Stationmaster .... Date

I hereby certify to have received the books, accounts, stores and other matters from Mr .... in accordance with the above certificate and have made myself fully acquainted with all regulations and special instructions in force for the working of the Station and am fully prepared to take charge forthwith.

Signature of incoming Stationmaster .... Date

As I finished this entry another set of papers arrived for me to copy into the log, and at that moment the resentment I had harboured earlier vanished and I would not have cared who made any entries in what I had now begun to think of as the railway company's book. I then started to write:

Duties of staff

Grade	No. Hours of duty		Breakfast		Dinner		Tea		No. of hours on duty
	On	Off	From	To	From	To	From	To	Hrs mins
	am	pm	am	am	pm	Pm	pm	Pm	
Station-Master	8.00	9.48	8.30	9.00	1.00	2.00	5.00	5.30	11.48

Detail of Duty

The officer in charge must see that each of his staff fully understands the duties allotted to him, that each is capable of performing such duties, that a list of such duties is from time to time posted so as to be easy of access and that the men may have it continually before them. To visit all Signal cabins or cabins daily and by actual examination satisfy himself that all general and specific instructions and advices are duly and properly carried out and that same are on hand and carefully preserved, to sign line-clear books at time of visit, to meet all trains during time he is registered on duty. To inspect daily all Rooms, Offices, Lavatories, Closets, and Urinals and see that they are in every respect kept clean and that the latter are kept flushed throughout the day. To see that all legal notices, timetables etc., are carefully and conspicuously exhibited and renewed from time to time as required and that no other than those authorised by the company are exhibited at the Station. To see that the distribution of gratuitous timebook, covers and timetables is duly and properly made to the various Hotel and private and public Offices and by personal visits satisfy himself that the Regulations of the Company are carried out in this respect. To see that the Company's arrangements for the conveyance of Passengers and Parcels by rail are duly and properly announced and that the Company's business is in every respect carried out satisfactorily by the Agent, both in dealing with the Goods and Parcels.

To personally receive all cash on behalf on the Company's business and see that the staff hand over all cash collected by them, daily before going off duty and remit same in accordance with the Company's Regulations.

To attend personally to all correspondence from the Public and Chief Offices and see that the general correspondence is promptly dealt with daily.

To personally prepare and sign all Returns and Accounts (after examining them) and despatch them on the appointed dates. To be responsible for the safe custody of all cash received, and satisfy himself that no cash is left in insecure places and on no account to keep cash over from one day to another without special authority. To see that all circulars and advices are properly noted by all concerned, carefully packed into the various Guard books and indexed for reference.

Duties of staff (continued)

Grade	No. Hours of duty		Breakfast		Dinner		Tea		No. of hours on duty
	On	Off	from	to	from	to	from	to	Hrs mins
	Am	Pm	am	am	pm	pm	pm	pm	
First Week 1									
Porter 1	7.15	7.15	8.20	8.50	12.45	1.45	4.15	4.45	10.00
Second week	9.30	9.30 *			12.45	1.45	4.15	4.45	10.30
First week									
Lad Porter 2	7.45	7.30			11.40	12.40	3.45	4.15	10.15
Second week	8.10	8.20			11.40	12.40	3.45	4.15	10.40

* or until departure of last train

Detail of Duty

Porter

> To assist generally at the Station as per detailed duty sheet.
> Relieved for meals.
> No Sunday duty.

Lad Porter

> To assist generally at the Station as per detailed duty issued by the Stationmaster.
> No Sunday duty.

The specific duties that we were expected to carry out, and those allotted to undertake them were also listed:

Details of Special duty (sic) *and table*

Details of work to be performed	*Porter to perform works*	*Time worked*(sic) *to be performed*
Station platform	*1*	*9.00am - 10am*
(later amended to platforms)		
Lamps Cleaning	*2*	*9.30am - 10.40am*
Lighting	*2*	*various times*
Footbridge	*nil*	
Glass	*1 & 2*	*when required*
Closets & Urinals	*1*	*7.00am - 8.00am*
Offices & Waiting Rooms	*1*	*7.00am - 8.00am*
Weighbridges		
Booking Halls sic.	*2*	*7.00am - 8.00am*

That was the last entry that I made in this book. From then on it was the responsibility of the Stationmaster and his successors, to ensure that it was kept up to date. I believe that the same book was still being used in the office when I left the railway station.

Although I was glad to have finished that task, one unexpected bonus was that afterwards, although I was the newest member on the staff, everybody, except the Stationmaster, came to me if they had queries over the Rules and Regulations, because they assumed that I would know the answer.

+ There are entries in this same book as late 1923, so the book was in use for almost 50 years. In the appendix at the back of this book you will find copies of later instructions and inventories, that appeared.

ALL CHANGE

A fortnight after I joined the railway my uniform arrived. As soon as it arrived I was despatched, to the 'Gentlemen's' and after making sure that no passengers were using the facilities, was told to get changed, so that at last I looked like a proper railwayman. The uniform was made of heavy serge and at first it was very stiff and uncomfortable, but after a while I got used to it. The full outfit consisted of a cap, jacket, waistcoat, trousers (2 pairs), boots, and an overcoat, all of which, I was informed, had to last me twelve months before I would get any replacements. I also had to wear a collar and tie. I had never worn a tie before in my life before and had to be shown by Bob how to tie it. On the way home that night I dropped into the local for a quick half, just to show off my new uniform.

Shortly after I joined the railway a number of changes took place, some big, some small; some on the railway, some in the countryside. On the railway the first change to occur was when the Bristol & Exeter Railway was taken over by the Great Western Railway in 1876. The first indication that we had of any change was a notice in the porters' room telling us of the changes, and informing us that our Conditions of Employment, the Rules and Regulations, and our wages, would remain the same, at least for the time being. Later some changes were made, but the Rules and Regulations, and Terms of Service, remained much the same. Later still, a medical fund and pension scheme, both of which we had to pay for ourselves, were started. Slowly new wagon labels, passenger tickets, and luggage labels started to arrive at the station. Engines, carriages, wagons, and trucks with B&E or Bristol & Exeter Railway on their sides were slowly replaced with those bearing GWR or Great Western Railway.

In the countryside, shortly after the line opened to Minehead, large livestock markets were set up at Washford, Minehead, and Taunton. The farmers soon realised that if they sold their animals at these markets the buyers, rather than themselves, paid for the animals to be shipped to their final destination. It was not long before livestock movements through our station almost dwindled away to nothing with just the occasional shire horse for farm work, or a cob for the carrier's cart and other horses for the carriages of the local gentry, or for point-to-points, or hunting, being loaded into horse boxes. Sometimes on hunt days if the meet was some distance away, the members of the hunt would bring their horses to the station, so that they could be taken to the meet, by rail.

The changing pattern of traffic on offer meant that we were kept as busy as ever. Until the coming of the railway the farmers simply produced enough to satisfy their own needs and the needs of the immediate area. They very soon realised that they could now supply greater quantities of produce of all kinds, and it could be shipped by rail to the big towns within twenty four hours. In the past, farmers' wives had turned any surplus milk they had into butter, cheese, or cream, and although some ladies kept their hand in by making these products for their own use, or to take to the local market, many farmers now shipped all their milk to the large dairies in the towns, and if the diaries had any surplus they turned it into dairy products themselves.

Soon we all became adept at rolling two loaded (17 gallons) milk churns at a time, (one in each hand) along the platform to the point where they would be loaded onto the train. The station cat soon learnt what was in those churns, and as soon as he heard the noise that they made as they were rolled along the platform, he would appear and keep a beady eye on the proceedings. If by any chance a small drop was spilt on the platform, he was there in a flash to lick it up.

As I mentioned earlier, some of the farmers' wives took their wares up to town on market days, normally travelling up on the 8.10am train. However, I soon noticed that one farmer was in the habit of sending his daughter up to town on market days. She was rather pretty, and shy, and I soon realised that the only chance I stood of her even noticing me would be if I managed to reach her first as the train came in, and to help her, and her packages, onto the train. As I was the youngest and the fastest on my feet, I always managed to get there first to help.

After a while my efforts were rewarded with a pretty smile. Later in the day she returned on the train that arrived back at Bishops Lydeard at 4.10pm. Although I was still on my tea break I would make sure that I had finished my 'snap' (food) before the train arrived so that I could see her as she got off the train, and perhaps get another smile. It was impossible to talk to her because Mr Elliott was always around, and he considered that railway employees were not paid to stand around to talk to very pretty young ladies.

One day I had been sent out to deliver a small parcel to one of the houses down the lane and because I had been delayed, whilst the lady found her purse, to give me a tip for my efforts (3d) I was rushing back because I could hear the 4.10pm train departing from the station. Suddenly there was the lady I was rushing to see, walking up the station drive. She gave that wonderful smile and said to me that she was surprised not to see me on the platform when the train arrived, and was worried in case I had had an accident or that I had been taken ill.

I tried to explain what had happened, and at first got hopelessly tongue-tied and then became flustered before I finally managed to explain what had happened. After we talked for what seemed like just a moment, but was probably five minutes or so, I had to make my apologies and dash back to the station before Mr Elliott noticed that I had taken rather longer to deliver the parcel than I should have done.

In the meantime I had found out that her name was Amelia and that everyone called her Amy; that she was nineteen years old, and she lived on a smallholding near the village of Halse. As we parted I said that I hoped that I would see her on market day next week. I thought that my mates had not noticed that I had fallen for Amy's charms, but when I got back, they all took a great delight in informing me that she had appeared to be quite put out when I was not on the platform to help her off the train. I did not let on to them that I had seen her, and had also spoken to her when I had met her down the road.

The next market day I arrived early at the station, signed on and started to do my work, in the hope that if she arrived early I might be able to pause, and talk to her again, if

Mr Elliott was not around. I was thrilled when she arrived long before the train was due, even before Mr Elliott came on duty and so we managed another snatched conversation before he arrived.

When the train arrived I handed the parcels to her in the train, shut the door; the carriage window came down, and she leaned out. Thinking that she was going to say something to me I leaned forward, and received not only a wonderful smile, but also a brief kiss. Fortunately our Stationmaster was looking the other way at the time; I am sure that he would not have approved.

Eventually our meetings developed into courtship. In the meantime, traffic offered at the station continued to increase, as did the variety of goods on offer. Day old chicks (alive); rabbits (dead); braces of pheasants in the shooting season; sometimes even fish caught in the local rivers, either to be stuffed and put into glass cases, if big enough or to be eaten by relatives or friends of the fisherman who he hoped would be impressed by his prowess. Potatoes, swedes, turnips, parsnips, broccoli, carrots, lettuces and even strawberries, together with cut flowers, were all sent in season. Another traffic offered was fleeces (sheep); this was a job we all dreaded, because they had to be tied up in bales, which was very hard, heavy, and greasy work. After they had been despatched, the smell of lanolin, in spite of our efforts to scrub it away with carbolic soap, seemed to linger everywhere.

Hides and leather products were another important source of income for the station. Although at first more goods were sent away from the station than were received, after a while the slowly improving prosperity of the locality meant more materials were coming into the area than were going out.

Not all the changes taking place were of benefit to the local community. Large factories in the Midlands could mass produce many iron and metal worked items much more cheaply than the traditional source, the village blacksmith, who, though reduced to repairing items of metalwork, or one-off items, and of course making and fitting horse shoes, normally managed to make a reasonable living. Local tanneries also suffered, when large factories like Clarks of Street were established in the county producing thousands of shoes, with leather they had tanned themselves. In time these factories employed far more people than ever the individual cobblers ever did, and so while the community as a whole prospered, the local craftsmen did not.

Some small traders did benefit. The number of small shopkeepers grew considerably, selling not only traditional items; you would also find nails on sale in the hardware shop. They had previously been hand made locally, but were now being mass-produced, instead of being made to order, by the local blacksmith. Other items that the countrymen had not even been aware of, but that their wives now considered essential, like mangles, were also for sale in the village ironmonger's shop together with coppers, washboards, tin baths, and numerous other items.

Factories often opened alongside railway lines, and with direct rail links the railway companies were able to distribute their products in larger quantities, more quickly and over a wider area than ever before. Because they were producing greater quantities their goods became cheaper. Their products even found their way into to the village stores giving the country folk a chance to buy goods only seen in the towns up to that time.

Small printers also started to produce local, mainly weekly, newspapers; national daily newspaper publishers in London found that the railway could distribute their newspapers all over the country by the following morning. Because more people could read and write, the postal service grew. Again the Post Office depended on the railway to get their letters to all parts of the country by the following day. These services needed a Post Office / newsagent in most villages to sell their products to the public.

The growth of large factories producing clothing and materials for both ladies' and gentlemen's requirements resulted in the appearance of both ladies' and gentlemen's outfitters in all the large towns, and even in some of the larger villages. All these producers depended on the railway to distribute their products and so we were kept busy trying to meet the needs of the local community.

We thought that there was nothing new for us to handle, until one day two ploughs arrived on separate flat wagons with the local pick up goods train one morning. They were unlike anything we had seen before; they were all metal, instead of being wooden except for the plough share; instead of the ploughman walking behind and guiding it, there was a seat for him to sit on and a steering wheel.

We had to use the newly installed hand operated hoist to remove the ploughs from the trucks. It was the first time I had used this device and having lifted the equipment about a foot off the wagon, my hands slipped on the metal handle; the unit crashed back onto the wagon, and as it did so the handle spun back. Because I was standing too close it caught my waistcoat and quickly removed every single button.

Everybody laughed, but I was only the first victim of this contraption, and it was not long before we all became accomplished at sewing waistcoat buttons back on.

Whilst we were still getting our breath back after our exertions in unloading the ploughs, we heard the noise of what appeared to be an approaching steam engine.

As no train was due we were rather puzzled so dashed out and looked down the track to see this unscheduled train's arrival. Suddenly we realised that the noise was not coming from down the track, but down the road from the village. Just in time the drivers realised that the contraptions were far too heavy for the bridge that took the road over the railway line and at the last minute turned them into the area on the opposite side of the track to the station platform. After parking the devices they proceeded to drop the fire in the firebox, then strolled across the tracks and climbed onto the platform, to the fury of Mr Elliott, who admonished them for not checking if a train was approaching, or crossing by the road bridge.

One of the drivers informed our stationmaster that these steam ploughing engines (for that is what they were), had been built by a company called Fowlers at Lincoln, and unloaded at Taunton, because we did not have a large enough crane to lift them (they weighed 20 tons each). He told us that the contractors that had bought these monsters had been informed, by letter posted that day, that the two engines together with the ploughs that had already been delivered to us, would be available for collection by their representative, from Bishops Lydeard station the following day.

The next day dawned bright and sunny, and at about 9.30am two men from Geo. Weekes, the contractor, arrived and promptly set about lighting a fire in the firebox of each machine. Whilst one stayed by the machines to ensure that there was enough water in each of the boilers, the other wandered across to talk to us, thereby incurring Mr Elliott's wrath on two counts; by crossing the tracks, and distracting us from our jobs. But as the company the man worked for was a very important customer of the railway our Stationmaster had to try to contain his fury.

As we had never seen anything like these two machines before we asked how they worked. He explained that the two machines worked together, one on each side of the field and by means of a winch underneath the engines they pulled the two ploughs across the field together, both ploughs travelling in opposite directions. We said we thought it was a very expensive way of doing the ploughing, but he astounded us all by explaining that these machines could plough twenty acres a day, compared with just the one acre a man and horse could do in the same time.

When steam had been raised, the two steam engines set off back to their yard, and shortly afterwards two flat wagons each pulled by four horses arrived to collect the ploughs and take them back.

Thinking about these events afterwards I realised, as others had probably done already, that if the contractors to the farmers were prepared to spend such large sums of money on equipment like this, the farmers themselves must be recovering from the recession that had bedevilled them and the surrounding communities since the 1850s. After further thought, I realised that the first signs of recovery had occurred shortly after the railway had opened and furthermore, investing large sums of money like this could only mean that the contractors thought that the farmers and all the local suppliers who were so dependant on them, were all about to enjoy a period of relative prosperity.

I also remembered, with a wry grin that I, like many others, had thought when the railway was being built, that it would not have any impact on our lives. Little did I realise that it would shortly be largely responsible for further changes in my lifestyle.

WEDDING BELLS

Further thoughts led me to realise that short conversations, and quick kisses on the platform, when Mr Elliott's back was turned, would not enhance my courting, (for that is what I fondly hoped that it was) very much. Following yet another brief market day meeting, I decided that I could not possibly wait another week before I saw Amy again, and whatever the weather was doing next Sunday (my only day off work each week), I was going up to her house to see her.

Sunday eventually arrived. I was up early, and after polishing my boots until they shone, I shaved carefully, washed, combed my hair, (several times), donned my best (only) trousers and jacket and a tie. After a quick breakfast I set off for Amy's house. The weather was warm for April.

When I arrived in the lane leading to her house, my courage deserted me and I just could not summon up enough courage to go up the track to her front door and knock. As I walked up and down the lane I wondered if she had mentioned me to her parents? Suppose they did not approve of me? Would her father run me off the farm with his shotgun, and stop Amy going to market so that I would not be able to see her again?

Stroking the muzzle of a horse that had poked his head over a gate bordering the lane to see who was walking up and down, I was discussing my problems with him, because I thought that he at least was glad to see me. Suddenly from behind me, a voice said, "I thought perhaps you had come all this way to talk to me, not to Dobbin." As I turned Amy was laughing gently and once again I was reduced to a blushing stammering idiot.

She gently took my hand and we started to walk down the lane away from her house. She told me that her mother, who had been making the bed upstairs, had called down to Amy when she was washing up the breakfast dishes, to say, "That young man from the railway station is walking up and down the lane: I wonder why he has come along here?"

I soon realised that Amy had inherited her Mother's impish sense of humour. She told me they had watched me going backwards and forwards along the lane, until her Mother implored her to go and see me to put me out of my misery.

As we talked I realised that her Mother knew me, because after Amy had mentioned me to her, she had called in at the station on a number of occasions, in her nice new trap, (another sign of the improving fortunes of farmers?), to ensure that, as Amy put it, "I was a suitable person to see Her Daughter." Once Mother had approved of me, they had been wondering how long it would take me to summon up the nerve to call.

It also appeared that one of her older sisters, who was married, also knew me, because she often travelled by train from the station. Once her sister became aware of how Amy felt about me, she would tease Amy by complaining that, although I was always polite and helpful, I never seemed to be in such a hurry to help her, as I was to help Amy. I was beginning to realise that I would have to behave myself at all times if I was to remain in Amy's good books because members of the Pearce family seemed to be everywhere.

After we had been walking and talking for a while, Amy decided that it was time for her to turn about and head back home. As we did so we managed to kiss for the first time without worrying whether Mr Elliott was looking.

When we arrived back at her gate, she asked what I had planned to do for the remainder of the day. I replied that I had wanted to see her so much that I had not thought of doing anything else! She laughed again and asked me if I would like to come in for dinner. I replied that I could not do that because her Mother was not be expecting me. Laughing even more, she exclaimed that her Mother had been making preparations for me to come in for dinner ever since she had seen me in the lane that morning.

The meal was wonderful, and I found myself thinking that, if her Mother passed on her cooking skills to Amy before she got married, I would be a very lucky fellow indeed. After the meal was finished and the ladies departed to the kitchen, I was invited to join her Father in the Parlour. After we sat down, he took out his pipe and in silence, proceeded to fill, and then light it. Once he was finally satisfied that it was well alight, he started to question me about my family, and then about the work I had done in the past. He seemed pleased to learn that I knew something about farming. He then he asked me what my future prospects were.

I replied that I did not think that I could ever make the grade of Stationmaster. At present the prospect of improving my position appeared to be limited, due to the fact that advancement to another grade on the railway often meant being prepared to move to another area, and that for obvious reasons I did not wish to do at this moment. Fortunately I was spared further interrogation, when the ladies returned to the room. Mrs Pearce admonished her husband for smoking in the house, (which he appeared to ignore) then having opened the windows to let the smoke escape; we went on to talk about more general matters.

The afternoon passed very quickly, and after tea, (another wonderful meal), the time came for me to go home. Amy walked back part of the way with me. As we parted we kissed again, and she made me promise to come up to the house the next Sunday and not waste half the morning walking up and down the lane. From that time on, apart from when I took Amy home to meet my parents, (who were enchanted with her), I spent every Sunday at her house.

Sometimes we went for walks; occasionally her Mother would let her use the trap, and we would go up into the Quantock hills for a picnic. I was also happy to help with the harvesting when asked, because, although it meant us being apart for most of our precious Sunday, we did manage to spend a few minutes together in the shade of the haystack, when the women brought up pasties and the cider for our break. It also meant that I could earn a little more money for Amy to buy things for her 'bottom drawer'. We also continued to see each other on market days.

We were so wrapped up in our own world together, and were certain that we wanted to get married as soon as we could get together enough money, and somewhere to live, that it came as quite a shock when one of Amy's girlfriends asked us when we were going to announce our engagement, because to be honest we had not thought about it. The first hurdle to be overcome was to ask her father for his permission to marry his daughter. Once again, my nerve failed me that following weekend, even though I seemed to get on quite well with her Dad.

Amy finally grabbed my arm and having told me, "It's all right, he won't eat you," opened the door of the room in which her Dad had been patiently sitting waiting, pushed me in and promptly shut the door behind me. I managed to blurt out the question, at which point my future Father-in-law burst out laughing and said, "Son, I wondered when you would eventually get around to asking!"

The next problem was getting the engagement ring. I could not get time off from work without losing a day's pay, and as money was not too plentiful, I did not want to do that. The problem was overcome when Amy's Mum said she would go into Taunton with her to choose the ring she wanted. The next market day (no point in giving the Railway Company two lots of fares if you could manage to avoid doing so) they both turned up at the station, and I gave Amy all the money that I could spare for the ring.

Later that day they returned on the usual train, and after I had helped them both off the train I was shown the ring, which was still in the box (where it remained until the following Sunday when I went to her house to slip it on her finger). She assured that it was the very one that she wanted, and yes, I had given her enough money. It was only years afterwards that I found she had used some of her own money to make up the shortfall.

A couple of months later it was Amy's 21st birthday, and there was to be a special party to celebrate. As she would be involved in the preparations, I was told not to arrive until 4pm. On the Saturday before, I went into the village in my dinner break, to try to find a birthday present. I really had no idea what to get her, because all my efforts to find out what she wanted had only met with the response, "I would like a surprise."

The new ladies Haberdashery shop in the village seemed to be the best place to start looking, and when I explained what I wanted, the lady behind the counter, said she was sure that a nice lace handkerchief would be just perfect. It was not the sort of thing I would have chosen but she seemed very certain, and when I had paid for it she wrapped it in a box, and slipped in a card, "in case I wanted to write the lady a message."

When I arrived the next day Amy met me in the doorway and I gave her the present. She opened it immediately, said she was thrilled with it together with the message, and gave me a huge hug and a kiss to prove it. I took off my coat and whilst Amy was hanging it up, I walked through into the parlour. The first person I saw as I walked through the door was the lady who had sold me the handkerchief the previous day. No wonder she was so certain that 'the lady' would like it - she was Amy's Auntie.

It appeared to me that not only had the party been called to celebrate Amy's birthday, it also introduced me to all the members of her family. I soon began to realise that the Pearce family was even more extensive than I had imagined.

The next year, 1879, seemed to be our lucky year. In January I was made up to the exalted post of full porter with a pay rise of 2s 9d (14p) per week. In March, with the help of my future Father-in-law, we found a small two bed roomed terrace cottage in Bishops Lydeard, at a rent we could afford. Both sets of parents helped, giving us some of the larger items of furniture needed for the home, such as a bed, chairs and a table. In June, Mr Elliott reluctantly gave me a day off to get married in the local church.

The morning of our Wedding Day was cloudy, and there were frequent showers of rain. After midday, the clouds cleared, the sun came out, and it became very warm. Many of my relations were still living around Exford, and South Molton, and because of the distances involved had found it was impossible to attend. My youngest brother was employed as a footman at Cirencester Park, the home of Earl Bathurst and so he could not get there either, but my young sister, who worked as a housemaid for the Lethbridge family at Sandwell House had managed to get the afternoon off. As I walked up the aisle with my brother David who had agreed to be my best man, I noticed the packed pews fill with Amy's relations, but I was pleased to see that the three members of my family, all looking very smart, were not sitting on their own on their side of the Church, but that all of our friends were sitting with them.

Shortly after 2pm the organ struck up with the Wedding March, and shortly afterwards Amy appeared alongside me. Her sister Mary (the one who still complained that I did not rush to help her off trains) was her Matron of Honour and Amy's two nieces accompanied her as her bridesmaids. Amy, of course, looked absolutely wonderful.

After the ceremony we all walked to the village hall, and found that both families had helped to arrange a wonderful Wedding Breakfast. When the meal was finished, and all the toasts had been made, the men adjourned to the New Inn insisting that we went with them, because the ladies wanted to clear up the village hall.

When they had finished all the washing and clearing up, Amy's mother came in the trap to collect us both from the Inn. After thanking everyone who had come out to see us off we finally managed to get away, and as she took us back to our cottage Amy's mother surprised us both. She seemed to know just what we were thinking when she said, "I thought you would like to be alone," and dropped us outside our door.

As I opened the door Amy reminded me that it was my 'duty' to carry her over the threshold, which was finally accomplished after much laughter. I lit the range and put the kettle on for a cup of tea, whilst Amy went upstairs to change out of her Wedding Dress. Whilst I waited for the kettle to boil, and Amy to come downstairs, I noticed that while I had been at work, she had gone through the whole house washing, scrubbing, and polishing until everything shone like a new pin.

When she came downstairs the kettle had boiled, and I had made a pot of tea. As we sat drinking our cups of tea, I said how nice everything looked. Thanking me, she said that she had not realised that I could make such a good cup of tea. I explained that life on the railway had taught me some useful skills. She insisted on showing me all the items in the house that she had made herself, from the curtains, made up from material obtained from her Aunt in the haberdashery shop and sewn by herself, to the rag mats made from odd pieces of cloth.

The following morning I woke later than normal, crept downstairs, brought the range back to life, boiled the kettle, made a pot of tea, and took a cup upstairs to Amy. This was something that I had made up my mind I would do every day, once we were married. Having washed and shaved, I went into the garden, and whilst drinking my tea, enjoying the sunshine, I planned what vegetables I would grow.

Soon the delicious smell of frying bacon started to drift from the open kitchen window, and very shortly afterwards I learnt that Amy had indeed acquired all her mother's skills as a cook. Just before midday my father-in-law arrived, in the farm wagon with all our wedding gifts. As we carried them into the house Amy started to unwrap them and place them where she wanted them in the house.

After she had prepared and eaten a dinner that surpassed even her mother's wonderful standards, we finished unpacking our gifts, and after we had found the proper place for all of them in the house, we settled down to write our 'thank you' letters to all who those who sent us presents.

Once this task had been accomplished we settled down to enjoy a life of married bliss, where we could see each other each day, and not have to say goodnight before going home.

GOOD TIMES

After we were married the changes taking place at the station seemed small at first. During the Summer Amy would come down to the station with my 'snap' in her basket and if the sun was shining we would sit together on the seat on the platform, unless passengers waiting for a train were using the seats, in which case we would sit on the grass bank in the station approach, and spend my dinner break together.

Because Amy was no longer at home it meant that Mrs Pearce had to take the farm produce to market. Instead of walking to the station as Amy had done, her husband brought her to the station in the farm wagon, at the same time delivering or collecting any goods to, or from the farm. Sometimes Amy met her Mother, and they went together on the train into Taunton, to help each other at the market, or go shopping.

In 1881 our son was born. We named him William (after my father) Arthur (after Amy's father). Although we had been blissfully happy since we were married it seemed that our lives were now complete.

It was the same year that Mr Elliott obtained the promotion that he had striven to obtain for so long. He was moved to Stoke Cannon Station on the main line between Taunton and Exeter, which later, in 1884, became the junction for the Exe valley line which ran through to Tiverton. Having moved his furniture from the Station house onto the waiting train, we awaited the arrival of the new Stationmaster. We heard later, that shortly after he arrived in Devon, Mr Elliott met, and very soon married a lady from the nearby village of Brampford Speke.

Mr Campfield, our new Stationmaster arrived shortly afterwards, followed by his furniture, and family. The new Stationmaster was different in every way from his predecessor, both in appearance and ways. He was a family man, with a wife Rose and son Adam, aged seventeen, and also a daughter Henrietta aged twelve, who attended the village school. Adam was an apprentice fitter in the railway works at Newton Abbott and was only able to make infrequent visits to his new home. Mr Campfield himself was taller than Mr Elliott, about six feet in height, older, possibly fifty years of age. Although rather rotund, he could move faster than many men who were far younger, if necessary.

Although he was concerned with the day to day running of the station, (see log book entries in the appendix, regarding fire precautions, and shunting movements in the goods shed), he was far more concerned with the long term future of the station than Mr Elliott appeared to have been. He soon realised that with the exception of Stogumber the takings at our station were lower than at any other station on the branch line. Having been a GWR man all his working life he knew only too well that the company was always looking for ways to reduce costs, and introduce economies. Unless the revenue could be improved, with extra traffic, before long there would either be enforced economies (sackings), or the complete closure of the station.

After only a short period he realised that any major increase in revenue would have to come from new goods traffic rather than passenger traffic. This did not stop him from going round all the large houses and hotels in the area, finding out when guests would be arriving or departing, when children would be departing to, and arriving from boarding schools, and when families in the larger houses in and around the village would be going on or returning from their holidays. He would promptly offer them 'Luggage in Advance' facilities. If this offer was taken up it meant that we had to deliver or collect, often quite large quantities of luggage to or from their houses or hotels with either the sack truck or the four wheeled hand truck. We were happy because it meant that our income from tips increased considerably. He also made arrangements with a local firm to collect passengers from their hotels or houses by cab, and to deliver them to or collect them from the Station, an enterprise for which the railway received a small remuneration from the cab company.

The establishment of a factory making shirts on the outskirts of the village helped to boost our figures, with coal and cloth coming by rail, and the finished shirts being sent out to all parts of the country, but the prospect of further increasing freight traffic through the existing cattle pens, or goods shed was limited. His attention then turned to the area on the opposite side of the track to the station that had been cleared some years previously but not developed further. Making enquiries from traders in the locality, he soon discovered that goods destined for use in our area, were being unloaded either at Norton Fitzwarren or Taunton stations simply because we did not have the facilities to handle them. Similarly, goods from our area were taken to those stations to be loaded, for the same reason.

Amongst the local traders that he identified would use the facilities at our station if they were improved, were coal merchants (two); builders (three); thatchers; coopers;

wheelwrights; farming contractors; carriers (the last two for delivery of new machines and to send them back for repair if the contractor could not repair them himself); sawmills and the local slaughterhouse. Most of these enterprises would be despatching goods as well as receiving them and if successful it would mean that the future of our station would be more secure.

Armed with this information, he wrote numerous letters, and paid a number of visits to the District Office in Bristol. Finally he was informed that the work would be put in hand, and carried out in conjunction with the conversion of the branch line to the standard gauge, later that year, 1882.

A fortnight later, special trains, called 'permanent way' trains, stopped at the station one Sunday and unloaded quantities of rail; sleepers; chairs (that held the rails); fishplates; points; ground frames and ballast for both the sidings to be laid, and also for the conversion of the branch to standard gauge. During the following week copious amounts of oatmeal, and numerous barrels of ale, also arrived for the labourers who were going to undertake the work.

On the day before the work was due to start hundreds of labourers were brought to the branch in special trains. Although some alighted at Bishops Lydeard, the majority travelled further down the branch. Those who alighted drew their rations of oatmeal and ale, and dispersed along the line with the charge-hand for their section, to start preliminary work, before the conversion work proper started the following morning.

The following morning I set off from our house about 9.30am with our son Bill, who was now fifteen months old, to look at the work I thought would be taking place around the station. I was amazed to find that, apart from a permanent way gang installing the set of points for the siding south of the station, the whole line, as far as the eye could see, had been converted to the standard gauge (or narrow gauge as the GWR men would persist in calling it). It appeared that as soon as all the broad gauge stock, including engines, carriages and wagons, including 'cripples' (damaged) in various sidings, had been moved off the branch during the night, the labourers set to work. What was even more remarkable was that the gangs on our section were not able to start work until much later than those further down the branch, whilst they waited for the stock to arrive in, and then clear, the section.

When the line Superintendent visited the site to see how work was progressing, I heard the Clerk of the Works inform him that the whole line had been converted from Norton Fitzwarren as far as Nethercott bridge already, and the teams working from Williton and Minehead were also making good progress. The five hundred labourers completed the work that same day, and a standard gauge engine ran through to Minehead late that afternoon.

On the Monday checks were carried out by the inspectors, and once they were satisfied that it was safe to run trains over the whole length of the branch, they gave permission for normal services to resume on Tuesday. There was a slight delay after the conversion work was completed, and three months elapsed before members of the permanent way gang that undertook new track-laying work in the District, arrived to start laying out the new sidings, in February 1883.

Before the work was even completed Mr Campfield was visiting the local traders to inform them of progress and try to obtain new business.

When completed there were three lines in the sidings; number one siding which was the longest and the furthest from the running line, soon had coal staithes installed alongside the track into which the coal was quickly shovelled from the railway wagons. The two local coal merchants set up scales in the 'roadway' between this siding and the number two siding, to fill and weigh 1 cwt. (50 kilos), sacks of coal, which they then loaded onto their carts. Once their horses had been harnessed up, they set off to sell this coal to householders in the surrounding villages and hamlets. If the coal merchants did not empty the railway wagons quickly enough, they were charged 'demurrage' by the railway.

The number two siding was used to load and unload general goods and to assist with this work two cranes were installed, one of seven tons, and the other of ten tons capacity, in the roadway between the number two and three sidings. The number three siding had a run round loop to release the engine, and at the end of the head-shunt was a ramp made of old broad gauge baulk timbers and rail sections, (the GWR never wasted money if it could be avoided!), down which large-wheeled vehicles could be winched from 'flat' rail trucks to ground level.

The number three siding was not normally used to load and unload wagons or trucks, but kept clear, so that the engine could be released when it arrived with the morning pickup train. Once the loaded wagons had been dispersed and this track was clear, during the remainder of the day wagons that we had emptied and were to be returned empty to their originating depots together with loaded wagons were marshalled here to await collection by the same train that had called in the morning.

Once the engine had left we had to use 'pinch bars' or the coalman's horse if he was available, in order to move the wagons around the siding. All 'loose' wagons (those not attached to a brake van or engine) had to have their brakes pinned down to prevent them rolling towards the running line on the down gradient. The roadways between the tracks enabled road vehicles to draw alongside the rail wagon or truck, to tranship goods between road and rail vehicles.

All the points within the siding were operated by ground frames, and with the exception of those controlling access to and from the running line, and the 'neck' of the siding, were operated by those members of staff undertaking the shunting work. The sets of points on the running line, and the neck of the siding, together with two signals erected the to prevent trains running through the points when they were set for the siding, were operated from a ground frame that was contained in a small cabin.

To operate this ground frame Arthur Pillar and I were made up to the grade of signalman / porter, after we had passed the appropriate test. Another small but welcome pay rise. These were the only additional operating costs incurred in order to maximise the benefits of any increased traffic.

These improvements did not bring about the immediate large increase that Mr Campfield was hoping for, but the sustained gradual increase that did occur, together with events that were happening elsewhere in the country, were to bring fresh problems to the whole branch line.

"BUT NOW 'TIS ALL HURRY PUSH"

Until 1882, virtually all the vehicles that travelled on the highway had been horse-drawn, but things began to change quickly over the next decade. The first sign of the changes that were about to take place came when the daily goods train arrived one morning with two flat trucks immediately behind the engine. One contained what looked like a steam plough and on the second flat truck was a contraption, the like of which we had not seen before. The guard proceeded to put on the brake in his guard's van, and pinned down the brakes on four other wagons, before uncoupling the first seven wagons from the rest of the train so they could be brought into our siding.

Whilst this was being done I set the points for the train to come into the siding and pulled off the signal. The engine driver acknowledged that he 'had the road', and after checking that he had received the 'right o' way' from the Guard, drew the train slowly forward. As he passed me he checked to make sure that the number three road was clear, and to find out how we wanted the shunt to be performed.

After consulting the shunter, he was told to run into the number three road, and after sufficient brakes had been pinned down, to un-couple the engine, run round the train, and once the road had been reset, and the wagon brakes released, propel the stock forward, until the two flat trucks were hard against the new ramp. Once the brakes were pinned down on these two wagons, the remainder of the 'consist' could then be drawn forward into the siding. The brakes were then pinned down, the engine was released to go forward onto the running line to couple up to the remainder of the train and then, once the road had been reset and the wagon brakes released, it could then proceed on its way down the branch line.

Fortunately on this day it was not necessary to shunt any wagons into the cattle dock or the goods shed. Had this been necessary, they would have been marshalled ahead of the flat trucks. They would have been detached first and then drawn into number three road after the engine had run round, then been drawn back onto the running line and when the road into the shed had been set they would then have been propelled in. The engine would then have to carry out the procedure outlined above.

During the course of the day both units were slowly winched off the wagons and down the ramp until they reached ground level. When the contractor's men came to prepare the 'steam plough' before driving it away we found out that it was in fact a steam engine, and by means of an endless belt worked by a large fly wheel mounted on the side of the boiler could operate all kinds of equipment from band saws to threshing machines, which was the second item that had been delivered that day.

In the evening when the daily 'goods' arrived to collect the loaded wagons together with the two empty flat trucks the procedure was much simpler. Stopping to the north of the signal protecting the siding, he would, once sufficient wagons were pinned down, uncouple and draw the engine forward until it had cleared the points. When the shunting arrangements had been resolved, and the points set, he would back onto the wagons in the goods shed siding, couple up and draw them out of the siding until all the wagons were clear of the points. Then as soon as the points were reset once again they would be set back and coupled up to the remainder of the train standing on the running line.

The procedure would then be repeated until all the wagons awaiting collection had been drawn out of the siding and marshalled onto the train standing on the running line. Sometimes the driver could be persuaded to line up some of the empty wagons in the section of the siding where they were to be loaded, thus avoiding the need to use pinch bars or the coalman's horse. If the driver was running late we knew better than to ask!

The train was then free to proceed to Taunton, where all the wagons were marshalled into other goods trains travelling to all parts of the country. In spite of the complicated procedures, nearly all these wagons reached their destinations the following morning. Soon the steam engines on the roads were joined by steam lorries, and even steam cars.

Many of these vehicles were delivered by rail, because the unreliability of the vehicles, and the poor state of the roads meant that travelling long distances by road was not practical. When a little later automobiles started to arrive in the area they were also brought in by rail. This meant that our ramp saw frequent use, for the spare parts for these vehicles, together with the steam coal (domestic coal was not suitable); carbide for the acetylene headlamps and oil for the lamps of horse-drawn wagons, carriages, and carts. When the cars with internal combustion engines arrived, a lock-up store was built in the siding (see note in appendix) for petroleum products. Many people mainly of the younger generation, decided that they could not get about their daily business quickly enough by walking, and they purchased bicycles which at first went on sale in the hardware shop in the village.

The railway company itself realised that there was a need for increased speeds not only on the passenger, but also on the freight trains. This meant that the next morning delivery service could be offered over a wider area. The final abolition of the broad gauge over the whole of the GWR system further extended the range of these services. There was one unexpected benefit from these improvements for the local fisherman who used to go out in his boat, and then when came back to port, go round the local houses to sell his catch. He found he could get plentiful stocks of fish, and a greater variety, from North Sea ports like Hull the next morning, by rail. He promptly sold his boat, and opened a wet fish shop in the village collecting his day's supplies from the first passenger train that arrived in the station each morning.

The railway encouraged many large companies with various offers of assistance, to locate their factories alongside their main lines. Some of the companies soon became household names: Huntley & Palmers for biscuits; Lyons for tea, also cakes, and ice cream later; Walls for sausages, also later for ice cream; and Guinness. They were all helped by prompt deliveries by the railway, and constant advertising in newspapers, on hoardings and metal signs on the railway, and even on the walls of the very shops that were selling their products.

In addition to all the products already mentioned, the railway became involved in moving large amounts of material that had not even been available a few years previously. For example, a number of gasworks were built to serve the larger conurbations with gas for cooking, and for lighting the streets after dark. The by-products from these works were coke (for smelting ovens); tar (for surfacing roads); and benzene (for petroleum products). Although this development did not directly affect Bishops Lydeard, the gasworks at Williton and Minehead put still further pressure on the branch line, and it must be remembered that at every station that had a siding, the shunting arrangements outlined above had to be carried out, and whist the section was occupied, no other trains could pass up or down the line.

The increasing volume of traffic through the goods shed meant that arrangements had to be made to ensure the goods were cleared on a regular basis, rather than leaving materials lying around on the shed floor waiting for the customer to collect. A carrier was asked to act as agent and a careful note was made in the log book (see appendix) of the times he was to collect and deliver goods to and from the station, together with the commission he was to receive for undertaking this work.

It soon became obvious that before long, the volume of traffic on the line would outstrip the capacity of the line, unless major improvements were carried out. Because of the vast amount of capital required to convert the main line, from Paddington to Penzance, from broad to standard gauge, projects like this could not be carried out until that work was completed in 1892.

A BAKER'S BOY

We had always hoped that we would have a number of children but it was not to be. When our Bill was 14 he left school and managed to get a job as a van boy, with the local baker. There had been a small bake-house in the village for as long as I could remember, but until the railway came he had to rely on flour from the local miller, which was only sufficient to produce enough bread for a small number of local people. At first he sold his bread from a handcart going from door to door, but as word spread about the quality of his bread, people would buy their supplies from him as they passed through the village. Soon he found that he could sell so much bread that he had to keep returning to the bake-house throughout the day to collect further supplies. Furthermore, he had to get out of bed even earlier to bake the loaves.

Before long the local miller could not supply sufficient flour to meet the needs of our local baker, which meant he had to procure further supplies of not only flour, but also yeast, fruit, currants and raisins, and sugar from outside the local area, which, of course, arrived via the local station.

In an attempt to make life easier for himself he decided to open a shop in the village, because then his customers could come to him. Again, he found he simply could not cope with serving in the shop and doing all the baking himself, so he decided to employ his wife as an assistant to serve in the shop. For a while this seemed to be satisfactory, until he realised that he was not selling as much bread as previously.

Disturbed, he set out to find the reason for the fall in sales. He was sure that the quality of his bread was as good as it had always been, so what was the problem? He very soon found the answer. If he arrived on their doorstep with the smell of freshly baked bread arising from the basket on his arm, people were tempted to buy a loaf from him. If it was raining, very cold, or a long way to walk, they found it easier to bake their own bread.

Now our baker was a shrewd character, who soon worked out that if he went to the customer, his sales increased much faster than if he waited for them to come to him. His problem was that he could not manage to serve all his potential new customers from a hand cart, but a horse and cart would cost a lot of money. Many of his customers came from the nearby village of Norton Fitzwarren, and he reasoned that if he opened a shop in that village, customers who would not travel to Bishops Lydeard might be persuaded to buy from his second shop, and as supplies of bread had to be taken to those premises, he could then justify the cost of a new van.

He purchased the van from a local firm, and as William the coach-builder finished making the van he exclaimed, "'Tis a wagon I should never be ashamed to put my name on! Oak frame; elm sides all shaped and put here-right ... every piece of it 'tis a wagon that'll outlive you and I."

It was a small, four-wheeled van, two large wheels at the back, smaller wheels at the front and all the wheels had steel tyres. A canopy extended from the front of the van body over the bench seat on which the roundsman and vanboy sat, as far as the kick board in front of the driver's feet. It had two full height doors at the back, together with two sliding doors behind the drivers seat, from which the odd loaf would be obtained and handed to the van boy to deliver if the roundsman was feeling lazy, or if it was raining.

An unusual feature was a foot pedal in the well of the van (where the driver's feet rested) which operated wooden blocks which came into contact with the rims of the rear wheels when the pedal was depressed to act as a brake, slowing down both the van, and horse. In addition there was a pair of 'shoes' that would be placed under the rear wheels to hold back the van when descending steep hills. Finally, underneath the van at the back, were two hooks. From one of them hung the horse's nose bag, and from the other a bucket with a shovel which provided a very useful supplement to Bill's wages, whenever the horse provided a product for which many of the gardeners in the village (including me) were very grateful.

The body below the waist-band was painted in Prussian blue; the upper part of the van was finished in cream, as were the wheels and shafts, and the roof above the drip channel was finished in grey. In gold script on each side of the van, and across the back doors, were the words 'A. Smith Bakers & Confectioners'. A little grey mare of some fourteen hands, called 'Jess', was bought to pull the wagon. Bert (the baker) would tell any one who would listen that the van had cost him £34 15s 0d (£34.75) which included 300 hours of William's labour at 5d (2p) an hour. I often thought that he could have saved himself a few bob by not providing a metal step at each side of the van for his employees to climb up to their seats. As far as I was aware the step was never used the whole of the time he had the van; everyone climbing into the cab put one foot onto the hub of the front wheel, then the other onto the shaft, and reached their seat that way.

Shortly after our Bill joined the firm, Bert arranged to supply another shop in Bishops Hull, which he did not own, with bread and cakes on a daily basis, so not only were the van men busy, but Bert had to take on two more men in the bakery. It was often said that Bert Smith was the richest man in the village, and had achieved all this in the fifteen years since he took over the bakery from his father.

First thing in the morning, it was Bill's job to ensure that the horse was harnessed up, and hitched onto the cart. Whilst Sam was still loading the van, Bill would muck out the stables and put in fresh straw. Having made sure that the horse's nosebag was full, they would then set off for the local shop, and after the van was unloaded, return to the bakery and load up the van again, this time with the supplies for the shops at Norton, and at Bishops Hull. On the way back to Bishops Lydeard Jess would always stop for a drink from the stream that ran alongside the lane that crossed the railway line at Silk Mills crossing, and when she'd had her fill she would set off again at a steady trot for home.

On arrival back at the bakery, the first thing they did was to put the nosebag on Jess, and then go off for their own dinner. Upon their return it was time to load up again, and after dropping off further supplies at the shop, they would set off on their second round, through the village and the surrounding area. When they finally returned to the bakery in the evening, it was Bill's job to remove the horse's harness, putting Jess in the stable after rubbing her down, giving her a fresh supply of hay, and ensuring that she had enough fresh water for the night. Meanwhile, Sam would be unloading the heavy iron trays that the bread was loaded onto for the delivery rounds. Then he took the trays back in to the bakery for the loaves to be baked on that night.

The noise of the squabbling bird population was by that point intense, because they seemed to know that Sam's next job would be to sweep the crumbs from the van onto the cobblestones. As soon as the crumbs hit the ground, the birds would flutter down, and in no time at all the whole area was cleared.

On Sunday mornings, both Bill and Sam would go into work although they were not paid any extra. Bill would clean every part of the harness until it shone, and the brass work on both the harness, and the van, until it also sparkled. At the same time, Sam would be washing down the van and when he had finished that he would give Jess a good grooming, sometimes even plaiting her mane and her tail. When they came down to the station to collect supplies, everything was glistening in the sunshine; they looked a fair treat.

Baking bread was not the only source of income for baker Bert. At Christmas time many of the villagers would bring their poultry to be cooked in his ovens because the ovens on their ranges were simply not big enough. At Easter time the smell of Hot Cross Buns wafted through the village, and at a halfpenny each he managed to sell considerable numbers. Eventually with penny buns, bath buns, Chelsea buns, and wedding, birthday, christening and Christmas cakes to order, the confectionery sales became a very important side of the business.

Five years after Bill started work, Sam the roundsman decided that he would prefer to work as a drayman for one of the local cider makers. The pay was no better but he learned that most of the publicans were in the habit of slipping the drayman a pint when he made a delivery, so Sam worked out that he could save himself a few bob each week.

Bill was made up to roundsman and with it he got a pay rise of £1 per week. From the moment our Bill became a roundsman he vowed that he would not use the whip on Jess, as he said that she knew the work that had to be done, and would do it at her pace which was fine by Bill. So, the whip remained in the box on the van the whole time Bill worked with that horse. The only time it came out of the box was on Sundays when the brass ferrule on the whip was polished at the same time as the brass side-lamps.

His boss was unable to recruit a van boy to help Bill immediately. Although it was hard work our Bill soon used the absence of a vanboy to his advantage. He found out that young ladies could not resist the offer of a ride on his smart van if it was raining, or cold. It also worked when it was hot, because when Jess broke into a brisk trot the cool breeze on your face was quite pleasant. I did notice that it was only the prettier girls that seemed to get the rides though, (like Father like Son, I suppose).

After two months a replacement van boy arrived. He was called Tom and his father worked as a handyman / gardener on one of the nearby estates. He was short, 4 feet 10 inches tall; wiry (thin); tousle haired, with a cheeky grin and an infectious laugh. Although he was a good worker his lack of height caused a few problems, but Jess soon learned to drop her head when Tom came to fit her head harness and blinkers, or slip her nosebag on.

Although Bill made a special tool, a broom handle with a nail hammered in one end; to enable him to draw the trays of split tins, bloomers and cottage loaves from the front of the van to the back to be unloaded, Tom was still unable to reach the trays at the top of the van so, if it was possible Bill unloaded the top shelves, whilst Tom unloaded those at the bottom. All the time he worked with Bill he never managed to carry the trays in with one hand, by balancing one side of the tray on the palm of his hand, and resting the other side of the tray on his shoulder. Due to his lack of height, and reach, he always had to use two hands to carry the trays into the shops.

Nor did the presence of Tom hamper Bill's efforts to persuade the ladies to travel on the van. It became quite a common sight to see three people on the seat made for two, (Bill must have blessed the fact that Tom was so small) with poor Tom squashed against the side of the van and the lady sitting next to Bill. After a while I began to notice one particular young lady seemed to be getting a lot of rides, that Bill was shaving each night before he went out, looking very smart when he disappeared out of the door. I didn't mention anything to Amy because I was quite certain that she would hear Wedding Bells even if the event was still three years or more away.

One day when Bill was walking home after work he spotted a great cloud of steam in the street. As he got closer he realised it was the car the Lethbridge family owned: it had come to a sudden stop in the aforementioned cloud of steam. The chauffeur, who was employed to drive the car, had gone to the village blacksmith for help when the vehicle would move no further. Between the three of them they found the broken item and dismantled it, only to find that the blacksmith was unable to repair it. With the chauffeur steering, Bill, and Fred the blacksmith, pushed the automobile back to the smithy, leaving the chauffeur to walk back to Sandhill Park.

Whilst they were sorting out the problem, one of the locals amongst the number of onlookers who had gathered, was heard to exclaim, "There now, if a man had foretold such a thing, when I was a boy he'd ha' been put down as a fool!"

The next morning Fred brought the offending part into the station to be sent back to the makers of the car. The transaction had to be done this way because Bert had no idea what it was called, and so on the label was a note asking the automobile manufacturers to send a part 'like this' back to him at his address. A few days later the replacement part arrived, by rail of course, and that evening Bill went down to the Smithy and helped Fred re-assemble the car. When the chauffeur arrived the following morning he was amazed to find that it worked.

If he had spoken to any of the villagers beforehand they could have confirmed that the car was working well, because Fred and Bill had spent most of the night 'test driving' it around the village. The fact that neither of them had ever driven one of these contraptions before is best glossed over.

When the whole transaction was finished and Fred had been paid (and Bill too!), Fred was heard to remark that, "it seems that there's a lot more money to be made from those things, than there is to be made from shoeing horses."

Shortly after, one Sunday afternoon Bill came home with the young lady I had seen travelling so often on the van. Although he had only popped in to introduce her, and tell us that her name was Mary, my Amy would insist that they both sat down to tea. Later that evening, when Bill returned from seeing the lady back to her house, he was admonished by his

Mother, who said, "What must she think of us, with the place all untidy (it was spotless as far as I could see), and nothing on the table?" (We had sat down to watercress and cheese sandwiches and home made fruit cake).

After this his Mother started a two hour quiz, on Bill's intentions towards the young lady in question. It was at this point I found out that Amy had known for some time that he was meeting a lady but, in spite of all her efforts, she had not found out who it was. Because I happened to remark that I thought it might have been her, because I had seen them together a number of times, it was my turn to be told off for not saying anything to her.

The young lady, Amy realised, helped her Father and Mother in the local Post Office and newsagent, and the reason Bill had met her so many times was she did the local post round in the village and its surrounds. When they met after she had finished her long round, she was only too happy to accept Bill's offer of a ride home.

Her initial experience with us could not have been too traumatic because she soon became a regular visitor to our house.

J GLIDDON, having been appointed by Messrs. HORNSBY and SON, Sole Agent, in *Williton and the District*, for their celebrated

PLOUGHS AND THE NEW WASHING MACHINES,

Begs to inform Agriculturists that he has enlarged his Stock of their Ploughs, so that any of the various sizes may be had at any moment.

The new Washing, Wringing, and Mangling Machine will thoroughly cleanse very dirty articles and can be worked by a child.

J. G. can strongly recommend these Machines to Housekeepers and others, as the very best made, and will take them back from purchasers after one month's trial, if found inefficient.

. May be seen at work every Tuesday.

West Somerset Free Press advert. 1862.

TIMES ARE STILL A'CHANGING

After the completion of the gauge conversion in 1892, the volume of traffic travelling up and down the branch line continued to increase, without any improvement in the facilities to handle it. Not only were there increasing quantities of the materials I have already mentioned, like coal for the Williton and Minehead gasworks, but new products not previously handled. The farms were using many more mechanical devices, not only for harvesting but for planting crops, including seed potatoes.

Increased mechanisation in turn called for bigger ploughs and more farm carts to bring the crops to the stations. This required fertilisers, as well as feed stuffs for the increased herds, or flocks of sheep, which in due course meant that more livestock were sold in the markets which then required longer trains, to take goods down the line as well as bringing supplies back up the line.

In addition to the steam cars which had been around for a few years, increasing number of automobiles were starting to appear in the area. They also arrived by rail, together with the many spare parts necessary to overcome their frequent breakdowns, plus the petroleum products required to propel them.

Many of the passenger coaches were now lit by gas lamps, and gas tank wagons came through the station on their way to Minehead where the wagons were stabled to enable the gas tanks for the lighting in the passenger coaches to be replenished. The increasing number of roads that needed firm surfaces for the heavier vehicles travelling along them required more trainloads of stone to be collected from Crowcombe station. The increase in the amount of coal being mined in South Wales and elsewhere required greater quantities of pit props from Dunster. Farmers outside the area wanted large amounts of the famous Watchet lime, which was also used by builders.

Since the coming of the railway Minehead had started to prosper. Many new houses, which had previously been built of local stone, were being built of brick because the builders found it was cheaper to bring in bricks from outside the area. Instead of thatch it was easier to use slates, brought in from North Wales (the slate quarried in the Brendon Hills was unsuitable for roofing). Local sources of timber were not adequate to meet the needs for joists, floorboards, roof trusses, doors and window frames.

Now that all the new houses were connected to the mains for water and sewerage, we started to see large 'steam shovels' come through our station on the way to Minehead to dig the trenches, together with large quantities of earthenware pipes. Many of these new houses we were told had indoor toilets, and the pedestals together with hand basins and even plumbed in baths, were all delivered by rail.

Once the houses were occupied, the people living in them needed furniture which included everything from beds, chairs, tables and gas lamps, to carpet sweepers and gas stoves, all of which were supplied by the many new shops opening up in the town, to meet the increasing demand for these products. Again, all these items came in by the railway. The new houses in the locality were of course needed to house the steadily increasing population, which in turn meant more people were travelling by train, and so more passenger trains were required.

The number of passengers carried was still further enhanced by Mr Campfield's efforts (as well as those of the other Stationmasters on the branch) with 'Holiday Haunts'. This was a booklet which appeared every year, published by the GWR and listing all the hotels, boarding houses, and guest houses, in every town within the area served by the Great Western Railway. As soon as the new edition arrived each year, he would be off round the village and all the large houses in the area selling 'Holiday Haunts' at 2d a copy.

At the same time he would enquire when they were planning to go away on holiday, and would also tell them of the 'luggage in advance' service. As soon as he had discovered where they were going he would pop a note through their door advising them of the best train to catch, where they should change trains, what time they would arrive at their destination, and how much the fare would be.

Because the passenger trains were not to be delayed if it could be avoided, the goods trains often had to be shunted into sidings at various places along the line to enable the passenger trains to pass. This would sometimes happen a number of times as the goods trains progressed up the branch line, and so by the time it reached our station it was sometimes three or even four hours late.

Often when the train did arrive it had the maximum load that it was allowed to bring along the line. When this happened a special train had to be sent out from Taunton, not only to pick up wagons and trucks from us, but sometimes from Crowcombe and even Stogumber on occasions.

One frequent traveller from our station particularly missed by me, was my Mother-in-law. At almost seventy, she had become extremely frail and was unable either to produce the butter and cheese, or to take it into market. In the past whenever she went to market on her own, she would always remark, "I hope you are looking after that daughter of mine young man," as I opened the carriage door for her.

If she was accompanied by Amy, as I went to meet them she would remark in a voice loud enough for all to hear, "Amy, do you know this young man, my dear?" which would raise a smile from all those who overheard her and who knew her.

I believe that Mr Campfield also missed her because he would always be on the platform when he knew she was due to arrive and as she came out of the Booking Hall he would touch his gold braided hat and say, "Good morning ma'am," and enquire after her health. Although he paid her all this attention he never attempted to stop me from opening the door and helping them on the train, by undertaking this task himself. Now I come to think of it neither did any of the other porters.

Her daughters went to see her most days in turn, to clean and tidy up, and to cook for them both. If it was Amy's turn on a Sunday I would go up with her, and whilst she was busy I would read to her Mother, who seemed to appreciate this because, in addition to her other problems, her eye sight was also failing.

One day in 1899 a passenger alighted from the early morning train from Taunton, and the passenger train guard asked for our assistance in unloading the boxes and a case the passenger had with him. Whilst we were loading the parcels and case on to the platform trolley, we were surprised to hear our Stationmaster warmly greeting the new arrival. It was only then we realised that our visitor was Mr Campfield's son Adam, who was now based at Exeter, and had come to carry out the annual safety checks on all the cranes, and hoists, within the station precinct and adjoining sidings.

After Adam had completed all his checks and was waiting for the next train to take him down the Branch line to carry out the same procedure elsewhere, we were chatting and I found out that he was still a bachelor. I was surprised to learn that his sister had married well and was now a 'lady'. This helped to explain why we had not seen her recently, but we never did find out why her father had never mentioned, nor as far as we were aware had even attended, her wedding.

HARD TIMES

The twentieth century had barely started when on the 16th April 1901 my Amy arrived at the station out of breath, with a tear-stained face and promptly burst into tears again. Eventually I managed to stop her crying long enough to find out what had happened. Her eldest sister Jane had sent her son Alan around to our house with a note, to tell Amy that her Mother had died in her sleep during the night.

Amy was about to go up to her parents' house to see what she could do to help, and had run down to the station to tell me what had happened, and to ask me to meet her at her parents' house if she had not returned home by the time I left work. It was all so sudden and unexpected that for the rest of the day I could not believe that I would not hear again that laughing lilt of her mother's voice as she said, "Amy, do you know this young man, my dear?"

On the day of her funeral it rained all day, as if the very heavens were in mourning for her. The church was packed, not only with her own family but with also with her friends, and many of the people in the village, some of whom we hardly knew, who had come to pay their last respects. Because he had given me time off to attend the funeral, Mr Campfield was unable to attend himself, although I think that he would have liked to have done so. He did send a wreath, and on the attached card he had written, "We shall all miss your wonderful smile, and your laughter."

It was about this time that the GWR, in one of its rare moments of generosity gave some employees a week's paid holiday. This meant that Amy and I, with the help of our 'priv' tickets (privilege tickets that enabled railway employees and their wives to travel at a quarter of the normal fare) and 'Holiday Haunts', of course, managed to go away to Weston Super Mare for a week's holiday, for the first time in our lives.

Many of the older hands simply could not understand why they should be given this concession, and I was told of one labourer who had to be ordered to take a week off, and when he walked out of the door that Saturday night he still could not understand why anyone was prepared to pay him for not working. Next Monday morning the person who had been delegated to do this reluctant holiday maker's job in his absence went to look for his wheelbarrow, shovel and broom. Neither he, nor the rest of the staff, who were searching for a whole morning, were able to find them.

On the Monday morning that he returned to work his supervisor instructed the labourer who had been unable to find the barrow, to follow the returning reluctant holidaymaker to find out where he had hidden it. Unaware that he was being followed he went straight into the goods shed and unhitching a block and tackle that was not often used, he gently lowered the barrow and its contents to the ground from their position high up in the roof of the building. He then went about his normal work. When the Supervisor was told the story he laughed so much that tears ran down his face.

The following year, 1902, Bert Smith our baker realised that he was selling even more bread and cakes from his shop in Norton Fitzwarren than he was at Bishops Lydeard. Because the shop there was often very crowded, he decided to close the existing shop and open another that was larger and of a more modern appearance. Convinced that he could not sell any more bread in Bishops Lydeard but that there was the potential for a considerable increase in sales at Norton, he bought a house on the edge of the village at Norton Fitzwarren and, with his wife in the shop, he set about exploiting the possibilities of further expansion.

This meant that he needed a manager to look after the shop and bakery in Bishops Lydeard. He asked our Bill if he would be interested in the job. The flat above the shop, that Bert and his wife had lived in, was offered on a rent-free basis to Bill if he took the job. Whilst Bill was thinking this over, Arthur, my Father-in-law, decided that he could no longer cope with the smallholding, and that he would move out when the next Quarter day arrived.

It had been agreed within the family that he would move in with his eldest daughter Jane and her husband Adam on their smallholding. Now that their children had left home they had three rooms available, for him to live in. Furthermore, Adam was content to let Arthur bring the best of his stock along with him, and also agreed that Arthur could 'keep his hand in' on the smallholding whenever he felt like it. Apart from a few personal items, and his favourite armchair, he had decided to place the contents of the house, the livestock, and all the plant and equipment on the farm, up for auction.

Bill and Mary were still going out together and were obviously very much in love, but Amy thought that, at twenty-one years old, our Bill was too young for the responsibilities of marriage and managing the shop and the bakery. When Arthur discovered what Bill had been offered, and how our Bill felt about Mary, he told them both to come up to his house and choose whatever furniture they needed, which he would withdraw from the Auction.

When Amy chatted to her father about her misgivings, he told her that if she influenced Bill not to take up the offer, Bill might spend the rest if his life wondering if he could have made it. When Amy asked me my opinion I said, if Bill decided that he would try for it, we should give him all the help we could.

The lovelorn pair discussed things at great length, and they came to the conclusion that the offer of promotion would probably not arise again if he turned it down now. With Mary's experience of shop work helping her parents in the Post Office, if they were to get married they could be earning two sets of wages between them. With a rent-free flat, filled with all the furniture and gadgets that they needed, this was an opportunity that was not likely to be repeated.

As soon as Bert was informed of their decision Bill was given the keys of the flat, and the following Sunday Arthur arrived with the same cart (but a different horse) that had brought our furniture down all those years ago. As I helped unload the wagon and carry everything up to the flat the memories came flooding back. With a lump in my throat I found myself thinking that if Bill and Mary only found half the happiness that Amy and I had, they would be very lucky people indeed. After we had unloaded the second and last wagon load, Amy arrived and informed us that dinner was ready, and as we ate it, I found the memories crowding back again of that first dinner she had cooked for me all those years ago.

Having listened to their arguments, Amy soon realised that they were right, and once we had given our blessing, and Bill had obtained Mary's father's permission to marry his daughter, with far fewer problems than I had experienced all those years ago, they set about making the arrangements for the wedding.

The wedding arrangements were quickly completed, and after the Banns were read they were married four weeks later. This, of course, set all the village gossips' tongues wagging! Many more of my family were able to attend this marriage. Although my Mother and Father had long since died, my brothers and my sister were able to come with their spouses and all their children. As I had come to expect, the Pearce family was still capable of organising a rather special wedding breakfast in the church hall, and I had the pleasure of welcoming Mary into our family. Months later Amy and I could not help smiling when our gossiping neighbours realised that they had been wrong in their assumptions.

One of the first tasks that Bill had to do when he took on his new job was to make up young Tom to roundsman, and then find a tall vanboy to get the bread and cakes down from the top runners in the van.

Whilst all these events were going on, the problems on the railway, caused by the lack of adequate facilities to cope with the traffic on offer, continued. Towards the end of the following year a large number of officials from the various departments at the District Offices came to our site, and other locations along the branch line. After many lengthy conversations they disappeared, and for a while, nothing seemed to happen.

Because the traffic originating or terminating at our station had remained fairly constant and the problems we experienced were due mainly to through traffic I had assumed that we would not experience any major upheavals. For a while there were a lot of engineering trains proceeding down the branch, often on a Sunday, loaded with bricks; rails; sleepers; chairs; timber; slates; rodding; sets of points; signal posts; signals and all the other materials required when undertaking major improvements on the railway.

We heard that at Blue Anchor a passing loop, together with a second platform, had been installed, and also a signal box, plus the signalling equipment required, to break up the long section between Minehead and Williton, and so increase the number of trains that could travel through that section.

As soon as I heard that similar improvements were to be carried out at both Crowcombe and at Bishops Lydeard stations, I promptly put in an application to be made up to signalman (from signalman / porter) and submitted it to Mr Campfield, who promptly endorsed my application and forwarded it to the appropriate department.

Whilst I was waiting to hear if my application was successful I arrived at work one Monday morning to find that a work's engineers' train had called on the Sunday and deposited vast quantities of the material required to undertake the work of upgrading the station.

Shortly afterwards, Mr Campfield received instructions that I was to go to the signal box at Williton on the following Monday morning, and the necessary travel warrants were enclosed. Each day as I travelled to and from Lydeard station, it was possible see that a considerable amount of work had been carried out during the previous day.

The first casualty was the run round loop on number three siding; when completed, the running lines through the station would be used for this purpose. On the area where the loop had been situated a second platform was built. This would eventually become known as the 'Up' platform. A second line was laid between the two platforms which formed part of a loop to enable trains to pass each other in the station. To control all the points, the facing point locks, and the signals, a new brick-built signal box was erected at the south end of the new platform between the running loop and the sidings. Shortly before the new signal box was completed I had been passed out as a qualified signalman at Williton box.

Before we could operate the new box at Bishops Lydeard, the same Inspector who had passed me out at Williton also had to satisfy himself that I was competent to operate the new box. When this task had been completed the inspector insisted on visually inspecting everything to ensure that it was in working order even though the Signal & Telegraph Inspector had already checked and passed the equipment. He then insisted on ensuring that everything that I was about to sign for on the inventory, especially the tea pot (enamel); brushes; dusters; bucket (coal); buckets (water); and buckets (fire) were in the box and the oil lamps in proper working order. Only then was I allowed to send the appropriate bell code (5-5-5) to the signal boxes at each end of my section to inform them that the box was operative.

After I had set the road and 'pulled off' the signals for the first DOWN train to pass the box, I walked over to the 'down' (the original) platform to collect the 'Staff' for the

Norton Fitzwarren - Bishops Lydeard section (its pristine condition did not last long) from the engine driver. I walked back to the box after the train came to a halt in the station, informed NF that the section was clear, and asked for permission for the UP train to enter section; then I made the first entries in the brand new train register. My next task was to 'set the road' for the up train and pull off the 'boards' (signals). When it arrived, I handed over the 'Staff' for the NF - BL section, returned to the box, and informed the box at Crowcombe that the section was clear, then asked for permission to send the DOWN train through. Before I could pull off the signal and set the road for the DOWN train, the UP train started to pull away and I paused to check that all the door handles on the carriages were properly closed, and that the tail lamp was in position as per the instructions in the rule book.

After 'setting the road', and pulling off the boards, I again walked over to the down platform, this time to the north end and handed over the 'Staff' for the BL - Crowcombe section and as the train pulled out I again checked all the door handles and the tail lamp.

I had been so busy that I had failed to notice the stranger who had alighted from the down train. When I arrived back at the box I found him talking to Mr Harris the Inspector. I soon realised that my 'relief' had arrived. This was the other signalman who was going to work alternate shifts with me in the box. Knowing that he was due explained why Mr Harris had been in no hurry to move on to his other duties.

After Mr Harris had introduced us to each other I was asked to sit in the corner while Mr Harris explained the working of the box, and when the next trains crossed in the station, the signalman performed the same tasks that I had done about an hour earlier, under the eagle eye of Mr Harris. Satisfied, the Inspector set off to inform Mr Campfield that he now had two competent signalmen working at his station. As he left, he turned and informed us, that when he called again in a few month's time, he expected the box to be as spick and span as it was now, and to ensure that the tea pot would be full.

I found out that Sam Chivers had qualified as a signalman some four years ago and up to now, had been working in the box at Cadeleigh station on the Exe valley line. Being single and having no ties; when he learnt of the impending vacancy at our station he had applied and was successful in getting the job. He explained that he required some lodgings in the village, and asked if I knew anyone who could help.

I knew of a lady who had recently been widowed when her husband had been killed working on the railway. With two young children, she was finding it difficult to make ends meet. Because of the need to look after the children during the day, she could only work evenings in the shirt factory, when a neighbour came in to look after the children. Knowing that she had a spare room I gave him her name and address.

At this moment Mr Campfield knocked on the door of the box, and smiling, opened the door and asked for permission to enter. I replied that he could do so, providing he wiped his feet thoroughly on our brand new door mat before entering. He introduced himself to Sam and asked us what arrangements we had made to cover both the shifts. I explained Sam's problems and suggested he went off now to see what arrangements he could make. It would be easier if I did the early shift this week, and if Sam managed to get fixed up, he could then work the late turn.

I watched them both walk down the platform, and took stock of my new surroundings. The new box was a great contrast to the box at Williton which was smaller, built to the design of the Bristol & Exeter Railway when the line was first opened in 1862. Wedged between the station building and the water tower the box was in the shade for most of the day.

The contrast with the new box could not have been greater. It was roomier, lighter, with an unrestricted view of both the station and the sidings, and I could also see for quite a distance along the running line in both directions. An added bonus was the view of the countryside that stretched out before me.

I found that the coal allocation for the box, delivered once a year in October, had not yet arrived. When I went to collect the 'Staff' from the next UP train I left the bucket (coal) on the platform at the point where the engine stopped. On my return with the 'Staff' for the next section I found that the bucket had been filled by the footplate crew. By this means, I was able to keep the stove working until the coal allocation for the box arrived, and also after the allocation had run out long before the next consignment was due.

If you are wondering why I needed coal for the stove in the Summer, I should explain that the stove in the box served two purposes; in the Winter it kept us warm, and it also existed to ensure that the kettle boiled and the teapot was kept warm, all year round. A full kettle of hot water was available at all times not only for our own use, but sometimes, footplate crews would ask for hot water for a 'mash'. The provision of hot water for footplate crews working on shunting turns in the yard, ensured that we continued to get a plentiful supply of steam coal for our stove.

The kettle was soon boiling, and I had made the first pot of tea in the new box. Once made the tea pot remained on the stove 'stewing' for the whole time the box was open: when the pot needed refilling a handful of tea was added, and the pot topped up. The resultant brew turned the insides of our white enamel mugs and the teaspoon dark brown in a very short time but what it did to the lining of our stomachs I do not know.

By the time Sam came back, not only had I progressed on to my second cup of tea, but I had polished all the brasses in the box, and had made a start on cleaning the windows, between working the various trains through the Station. I was pleased to learn from Sam that he would be able to move into his lodgings later that day. After downing a cup of tea, and making some suitably rude comments over the quality of the contents, he picked up his luggage and set off to settle in to his new accommodation. Some time later he thanked me for my advice which he claimed was the best he had ever received. To prove his point he married the lady less than twelve months later.

When Sam arrived later that day, to book on duty, I had finished cleaning the windows, polished the handles on the levers, found the clean duster that had to be used at all times thereafter to pull them, polished the floor until it shone, and 'blacked' the stove. With the exception of the windows, which were cleaned weekly, this became a daily routine, usually carried out by whoever was on early turn.

Shortly after the alterations to the station had been completed Mr Campfield retired. To commemorate his fifty years of service on the railway, the officers of the company presented him with a clock. As he ruefully remarked to me before he left, now that he had reached the stage when for the first time in his life he was not ruled by the clock, he was presented with one.

This was the first time that I had not had to load the outgoing Stationmaster's belongings onto the special train that arrived to collect them, and as I stood at the window of the box I found myself remembering all the events that had happened since Mr Campfield first arrived. After that train had departed, he and his wife were waiting for the passenger train to take them into Taunton where they could catch the train to Exeter to enable them to live near their son Adam. I went down to wish him well during his retirement, and I felt embarrassed when I found he had tears in his eyes.

The incoming stationmaster was known to us, because he had been acting as a relief Stationmaster in the area for a time, and had covered for Mr Campfield when he had been absent on holiday, and this was to be his first permanent appointment. After Mr W O Morris and his family were installed in the Stationmaster's house, the removal being conducted in the by now customary manner, it was not long before he was doing his rounds.

Like so many of the managers appointed to positions on the railway recently he gave the impression that he had been in the Army. Every morning I was told that he went round the station building with the senior Porter by his side, running his finger along the tops of notice boards to check that there was no dust; ensuring that the brasses and the windows were cleaned to his satisfaction, and that the toilets and the platforms had also been cleaned.

From my position in the box I could follow his progress as he came along the platform to the box to ensure that the train register was up to date. It always appeared to me that as he marched along the platform, he thought that he was still on the parade ground. Mr Campfield had always knocked and waited if he saw that I was receiving or sending bell codes, and only when he saw that I had finished would he enter. With Mr Morris it was different. When he arrived at the box, he would come crashing through the door without knocking and then close the door with a crash that set all the windows in the box rattling.

After checking the train register and finding it to be up to date, he would leave the box closing the door with another crash. Although he must have realised this was a distraction he persisted in doing this for several months, and I had resigned myself to thinking that whatever I said it would not make any difference.

One day when my inspector Mr Harris had called to undertake his quarterly visit, after I had satisfied him that the box was being properly run, and he had said how impressed he was with our housekeeping, he sat down in the chair by the stove for a quiet cup of tea before going on to meet the next signalman. Because I was busy, and also answering questions from Mr Harris, I did not notice Mr Morris coming along the platform and at the very moment when Crowcombe were asking me to accept a train, Mr Morris arrived.

Whether he had not seen Mr Harris arrive, or whether he assumed he had departed, I do not know, but he checked the register, turned round, still not apparently having seen Mr Harris, and on his way out closed the door with another tremendous crash. Whilst I waited for Crowcombe to repeat the message which, because it was not one of the more regular codes, I was not certain that I had heard properly, the Inspector jumped up out of his chair, and followed Mr Morris out of the door.

After I had acknowledged the repeated message, which was 1-5-5 (shunt train in section to allow following train to pass ahead) I noticed that he had caught up with our Stationmaster halfway along the Up platform and they were deep in conversation for some time, before Mr Harris popped back into the box to inform me that he was now leaving.

What was said during that conversation I never did find out, but after that day Mr Morris always knocked and waited for either Sam or me to tell him to enter.

The following year Amy and I became Grandparents for the first time and Amy was round to Mary's house less than an hour after our grandson was born, to ensure that both Mother, and son, who was to be christened William Arthur John were fine, and that there were no problems. Because the bakery and the shop had continued to prosper, and sales were steadily increasing under Bill's management, together with Mary's assistance, Amy was often asked to baby-sit because Mary was needed in the shop as soon as she was fit to return to work.

This gave Amy plenty of chances to become the doting grandmother, and these opportunities were doubled when two years later we became grandparents again, when our granddaughter Mary Ann was born.

BAD TIMES

The period from 1909 to 1914 was amongst the happiest times that Amy and I had known, as we watched the grandchildren grow up. We had plenty of opportunities to play and picnic with them, but if ever Amy wanted a rest with the children she knew that she had only to bring little William down to the Station and he would sit for hours watching the trains go through. If Mr Morris was not around she would bring him up into the box to watch the trains, which he regarded as a special treat.

The summer of the year 1914 was mainly hot and sunny, when suddenly, without warning it seemed to us, the newspapers were telling us that we were at war. Soon after war was declared in 1914, many of the local lads followed Kitchener's call and joined the forces and were sent away for training. Amongst the first to volunteer was Tom, who was Bill's bakery roundsman. Bill tried to dissuade him from going, saying the War would be over by Christmas, and how would Tom's wife (yes, he was also married to one of Bill's customers) manage if anything happened to Tom. When he realised that Tom had made up his mind Bill suggested that he joined the Rifle Corps, because as he was so small they could use him as a 'pull through' to clean the barrels of their rifles.

Shortly after Tom joined up, the van boy announced that he was also going. Because there were only boys leaving school available, Bill had to rely on a sixty-three year old man, and a succession of school leavers to carry on with the round. In time, even the supply of school leavers dried up as the Army took even younger lads. Soon anyone who claimed they were eighteen years old was accepted, even if, in some cases they were as young as fourteen years of age; eventually Bill had to employ a 'van boy' aged sixty-six years old.

Many of the lads on the railway also joined the Army, and the shortage of people to work on the railway became so bad that the Government had to declare that the railwaymen were a 'reserved occupation'. This meant that, in theory, railwaymen could not be accepted into the forces.

But this did not stop railwaymen trying, and very often succeeding in enlisting in the Army. The situation became so bad that women were taken on by the railway, for the duration, to do jobs that, until now, had been traditionally done by men. We saw one or two women passenger guards and heard that women were being employed as engine cleaners, in signal boxes, and even on permanent way gangs. Every one was needed because the railway was so vital to the war effort.

An extra track was laid alongside the siding to the coal staithes behind the up platform, so that equipment for the troops billeted at Sandhills Park could be unloaded. We were also kept busy with troop trains embarking and disembarking troops for the nearby camp.

When he saw the increasingly long casualty lists, our Bill decided that he must do his bit and join the forces. Because he was married and because of his age (thirty-six), he could not be enlisted, so he volunteered. Both Mary and Amy pleaded with him, in vain, not to go. After he had made arrangements with Bert for Mary to carry on as manager of the bakery until his return, he went off to war.

Twelve weeks later he came home for a week's embarkation leave and informed us that he had joined the Army Service Corps, where he had learned to drive a lorry. In an attempt to re-assure both his wife and his mother he told  them that he would not be going anywhere near the front lines. He also said that when he returned home after the War, he would attempt to persuade Bert to obtain a lorry to do all the local deliveries.

Shortly after Bill had left for France, Amy's father died. This was completely unexpected because he appeared to be so fit; it was a great shock to us all. Although all his daughters attended the funeral with their families, for what, although we did not know it at the time, would be the last time that they would all be together, many others, amongst them our son Bill, could not attend because of the demands of war time. Arthur had also outlived many of his contemporaries. It was just as well that it was a small gathering, because the food shortages meant that the family was quite unable to arrange the normal spread they had always prepared for events like this.

In 1915 His Majesty King George V and Queen Mary visited the station. The visit was supposed to be a secret, but for many days before the visit, the sidings behind the UP platform were the scene of much activity and all the stock in the sidings was taken away, gravel paths were laid on the roads between each track, tall gas lamps installed, and the coal staithes covered with tarpaulins.

Mr Morris went to even greater lengths to ensure that every part of his station complex was spotless, that all the brasses were gleaming, all the fire buckets had the water in them changed almost hourly, and the litter bins emptied as soon as any rubbish was dropped in them. The stores van that arrived at the station on the Monday morning before the visit brought new uniforms for every member of the staff, which we were not allowed to wear until the day of the visit.

Huge crowds had heard that the King and Queen were coming, but they were all kept away from the station, and could not get any closer than the Lethbridge Arms. I was on duty when the Royal Train arrived on time at 6.10pm, and, as instructed by the various bell codes, I shunted the Royal Train into the number one siding, after the trailing points which had now become facing points, had been clamped in order to allow a passenger train carrying passengers to traverse them. Although I had performed this shunting operation many times before, I had never shunted such an important train, and when the operation was completed, and the train was safely berthed in the siding, I breathed a huge sigh of relief.

Mr Morris managed to get his own back on the lad porter Stan. He had caused our Stationmaster many problems over the past few days, because he was always missing when Mr Morris wanted him to clean the brasses or the windows again, even though on one occasion the windows had only been cleaned an hour or so before. Stan was given the task of placing the Royal Chamberpot in the appropriate position underneath the train, and then emptying the contents of same the following morning.

When darkness fell, although it was war time, the whole area was brilliantly lit by acetylene lamps. The train was guarded by armed soldiers all night, but no one left the train until the following morning, when the King and Queen alighted for a short stroll along the new gravel path.

I was not due to go on early duty the next morning but I signed on for duty much earlier than normal, because I had heard that the almost complete privacy which had disappointed so many people in the village was to be broken at 10am by the King's own command. We heard that he had sent for the village schoolchildren, accompanied by the Vicar, the Rev Whateley and the Headmaster, Mr Gornell and asked for them to be assembled on the UP platform opposite the Royal saloon coach.

From my vantage point in the signal box high above the platform, I saw the lines of children coming down the lane towards the station, and soon picked out our grandchildren, William and Mary-Ann, who like all the children, were appearing in their Sunday best clothes. Somehow most of them, including I am glad to say our two grandchildren, had remained clean and tidy. My only regret was that my Amy could not see the children, because no-one apart from those working on the railway, those accompanying the children and the children themselves had been allowed to get any closer to the Station than the Lethbridge Arms, an action that caused some resentment amongst the villagers.

When the children arrived, they were lined up in single file to face the train. When the King and Queen came out to look at the assembly, the children sang three verses of the National Anthem for the Royal Couple who, when the children had finished, then returned to the train

After the King had sent a message saying how much they both appreciated everyone's kind thoughts I was then informed, for the only time in my railway career, by an Army Officer, that I could now make arrangements for the train to proceed. This took some little time to organise as another train had to precede the Royal Train all the way to London, consisting of one of the new 'Saint' Class locomotives (never again allowed on the branch line), and four empty passenger coaches. As the train Royal Train pulled out of the sidings the King and Queen waved to the children who were still lined up on the platform.

After the train had gone we had to hand back the new uniforms we had been given for the Royal visit. Because the Statiommaster Mr Morris was one of the few to have spoken to, let alone to have seen their Majesties, he was able to dine out for several weeks at a number of the big houses in the area recounting his experiences.

Two years after the Royal visit, in 1917, I returned home in the late afternoon having completed an early shift. Even before I opened the door I could hear my Amy sobbing bitterly. Rushing in, the first thing I saw was a telegram lying on the table. As soon as I read the words, "It is with regret that I have to inform you ... " I knew that our Bill was dead and this was the reason for Amy's bitter sobbing. This was the telegram that had been sent to Mary and which her mother had brought round to our house.

After Amy finished crying, at first she refused to believe that Bill was dead, and when she finally accepted that he was, she convinced herself that he had lied to her about going to the front line. It was months afterwards that we finally found out what had happened. Bill had driven his lorry to an artillery battery some distance behind the front lines with rations for the troops and ammunition for the guns. Whilst the supplies were being unloaded enemy guns opened up on the battery scoring a number of direct hits, destroying three guns, killing eight soldiers, one of whom was our Bill, and wounding many others.

Bert at the bakery was almost as devastated as we were by the news, but knowing that he was unlikely to find any one as capable as Mary to run the Bakery, asked her to carry on managing the shop and bakery, at least, until the end of the war. This helped to solve Mary's money problems for the time being.

After the death of our Bill, Amy seemed to lose all the zest for life that had been such a factor in bringing us together all those years ago, and which kept us feeling the same way towards each other ever since. Young William noticed the difference in Amy, because one day when he was helping me in the signal box, unofficially of course, he asked, "Why doesn't Nanny laugh any more like she used to?" What could I say? I simply replied, "She is very unhappy these days", a reply that only resulted in further questions that I found it increasingly difficult to answer.

Just when I thought that things could not get any worse, an influenza epidemic swept the country. Many people who had been subjected to food shortages and were malnourished, succumbed and died. In the country we had not been subject to the same stringent rationing that people in towns had experienced as we could usually supplement our rations with supplies from nearby farmers.

When my Amy caught the Influenza bug, I thought that she would recover as she had always done when she had been stricken down with colds in the past. After three days she showed no signs of recovery, indeed she appeared to be getting worse, and when the Doctor came to see her for the second time, he was shocked to find out how ill she was. He arranged for her to go into the local cottage hospital, but he said to me when she was on her way into hospital, that Amy seemed to have lost the will to live. Two days later she died and then it was my turn to wonder if there was any thing left to live for.

When we buried Amy in a grave next to her Mother and Father in the village church yard there were three further open graves awaiting other victims of the flu epidemic who were to be buried that day.

Shortly afterwards the Armistice was declared and some of the lads who went off to the War started to come home. Amongst the first to return was Tom, the former vanboy and then roundsman at the Bakery. The cheeky grin had vanished for good after four years in the trenches on the Western Front. His hair was prematurely streaked with grey, and he now walked with a limp because of leg wounds he had received.

Another local lad to return from a somewhat different war was Arthur Smith, the son of Bert the Baker. Arthur had finished the war as a Captain in the Army and it was said that the nearest that he had been to seeing active service was from behind a desk at Aldershot.

Before the War Arthur had not shown the slightest interest in the family business, but due to his Father's, and Mary's efforts, it had now grown into a very desirable business. Bert would probably have handed over the business some years before had it not been for the war. Now that he was almost eighty years old he felt that he was no longer fit enough to run the business, and he asked his son if he would like to take over the reins.

Although Arthur knew next to nothing about the business, he realised that he was unlikely to earn as much elsewhere as he could from the bakery. He was determined that if he was in charge he would make a number of changes, and the first casualty was the horse-drawn van Bert had bought all those years ago and was still in good condition. In its place came an ex-Army lorry which was soon painted with the legend A Smith & Son on both sides and the front and back.

The next change occurred when he decided that he needed a new manager to run the business. Of course, the person he had in mind just happened to be an ex-officer colleague of his, who knew nothing about the Bakery business. Gratitude was a word that Arthur appeared not to know the meaning of, and so, at less than forty-eight hour's notice, Mary found herself without a job, and she and the children were out on the street, because Arthur needed the flat above the shop for his new manager

There was room for Mary and the two children with me in my cottage, so I invited her to come and stay with me. Although it meant we were a little cramped, it did mean that Mary and the children had a roof over their heads until she could sort herself out. The other advantage for me was that, for the first time since my Amy died, I had proper meals put in front of me when I got home from work, and very shortly I began to put on weight again.

This episode did finally have a happier ending. Before too long Mary got a job in the office of the shirt factory, and was soon earning more money than she would have earned had she stayed at the Bakery.

Still more young men who had served in the War were returning home, and the railway was required, by law, to find them jobs if they had worked there before they joined the forces. I realised that as I was now seventy years old, I would soon be told that my job was required for a younger man and that I would be have to retire.

One day I was called into Mr Morris's office to be told the news I had known for so long would come. Partly because of the earlier episode with the crashing door in the signal box, and as the signal box was off the end of the platform, I did not normally come into contact with him more than once a day when he inspected the train register. So there was an absence of the mutual respect and understanding that I felt had existed between the previous Stationmasters and myself.

It came as a considerable surprise to me when he went on to say how much he would miss me, and he asked if I knew that there was a vacancy for a crossing keeper at Roebuck Lane crossing which was just to the north of Crowcombe Station. When I informed him that that news had not yet filtered down to me, he pushed an application form across his table, telling me to think about his suggestion, and that if I decided to try for the job he would endorse my request. As I got up to leave the office he suggested that I should not take too long to make up my mind because once word got out, there would probably be a number of people after the position.

When I got home, as I sat down after my dinner, I talked over his suggestion with Mary. I pointed out to her that there was a rent free cottage with the job and if I moved out, there would then be enough room in the house, for her and the children who were quickly growing up. I was worried that I might lose contact with her and the children, as apart from one afternoon a week to go shopping, I would not be able to get time off to see them, but she assured me that she would bring them up every week to visit me.

With my pension of four shillings (20p) a week, for forty-four years service on the railway and the crossing keeper's wages of nineteen shillings and sixpence (97½p) a week, and the new state pension they were talking about, I decided that I would be able to keep away from the poor house. The following morning I handed in the application form to Mr Morris, and some three weeks later I was informed that I had got the job, which was just as well because I was by then showing my successor how the box operated.

When the day came for me leave Bishops Lydeard station I was presented with a watch, even though I was not leaving the railway service. Unlike Mr Campfield's watch I felt that mine would come in useful. I would not have any excuse for not opening the level crossing gates in good time. As I walked down the steps of the signal box for the last time I saw Mary standing on the platform. She had gone up to Crowcombe Station by train, walked to the cottage and had scrubbed it all through. Having dusted and cleaned it for me it was now spick and span.

The following morning, which was a Saturday, we all loaded the few belongings I would need on to the carrier's cart, and once Mary, the children and I had clambered aboard, we set off for Roebuck Lane Crossing cottage.

When we arrived Mary and the children set about unloading the cart, but the relief crossing keeper was anxious to hand over the responsibility for the gates without delay, and fifteen minutes after I had arrived, I was opening the gate for the first time. Shortly afterwards the empty carrier's cart set off on its way back to Bishops Lydeard.

Mary made sure that everything we had brought up was in its proper place, and that I had enough food in the larder until I could get to the shop. After cooking me a special dinner, Mary said it was time for them to go as she had to walk to the Station to get the next train back to their home.

It was my chance to help them, and give young William a surprise in return for all the hard work he had done for me. I asked them just to wait for a moment while I opened the gates for the 'pick up goods' that I could hear labouring up the incline. They were surprised when the fireman jumped down to lift off the milk churn of water from the buffer beam of the locomotive, where it had been sitting ever since the train left Williton. This happened to be the only source of water for the cottage.

After explaining the problem that the family had in getting back to Bishops Lydeard the fireman and driver decided they would run the train over the crossing, and would stop the Toad (guard's brake van) on the road so that Mary and the children could climb aboard. Once aboard the guard waved his hand and off went the family back to Bishops Lydeard.

So I settled into a quiet existence, at the same time keeping in touch with my many friends on the railway. One unexpected benefit that I had not anticipated when I had decided to take this job was the amount of coal that 'accidentally' fell from the engines as they passed by my cottage; this proved to be a useful supplement to my coal allowance.

FOOTNOTE

One morning in 1924 the footplate crew of the first down train in the morning approached the crossing gates at Roebuck and found them closed against the train. When there was no response from Jon to the blasts on the engine whistle, they stopped the train and went to investigate. They found that Jon had died in his sleep, aged 78, shortly after completing his 50 years of railway service.

We have followed a very ordinary working man, through the great changes which occurred during his life. As most people do, he experienced 'Good Times and Bad Times'.

Now R. I. P.

To follow the story of Jon's grandson William, and granddaughter Mary Ann, why not read 'Changing Times', by the same author, to be published soon.

APPENDIX

Details are given below of some of the other entries in the log book which could not be easily introduced into the text, but which I hope will be of interest to the reader.

Instructions to be observed in Cases of Fire,
and list of Fire Appliances:

The fire appliances at this Station are: 6 Buckets

In future the Officer in charge of the Station must arrange for not less than 2 buckets to be filled with water and for them to be placed in position accessible to anyone at any moment, and in readiness for immediate use in the case of fire during the night.

Should a fire be discovered during the night in or upon any part of the Station premises the man on duty (if there be one) must do his best with the appliances at hand to extinguish the fire and if necessary must go immediately to the nearest person resident near the Station premises to give an alarm of fire, and to obtain assistance: he must then call the Station Master or Officer on duty in charge of the Station to render any further assistance in his power to effectually extinguish the fire.

The Officer in charge will be held responsible for personally seeing every night before going off duty that the buckets are beyond all doubt filled with water ready for use, and also satisfy himself that each member of the staff is made fully acquainted with these instructions and that each man knows where the buckets are to be kept, and are to be found in an emergency.

If there is a local Fire Brigade in the Town or neighbourhood, in the case of an outbreak of Fire the man on duty must in addition to calling the Station Master or Officer in charge go immediately to the Fire Engine Office or to the nearest warning station or fireman (as the case may be) to give notice of the fire and to apply for prompt assistance.

A copy of these instructions duly signed by the Station Master must be exhibited in the Porters' room at the Station for the information of all concerned.

Signed W. Campfield
dated March 25th 1889

100

Amounts allowed Agent as Commission for Collection and Delivery of Parcels:

The following is the scale of Commission paid to the Agent:

On all parcels where the railway charge (exclusive of 'paid on') does not exceed

6d (2.5p)			*1d*
6d	*and not exceeding*	*2s 0d (10p)*	*2d*
2s 0d	*and not exceeding*	*3s 0d (15p)*	*3d*
3s 0d	*and not exceeding*	*4s 0d (20p)*	*4d*

and 1d for every additional 1s 0d

Dist. Supt. Cir. 356
dated 9.3.83

Times of collection daily are 10.30am

Times of delivery daily are 11.00am

Painting Platform Seats, Forms and Time Bill and Poster Boards

It has been arranged for all Platform Seats, Forms, Time Bill and Poster Boards to be painted at least once every two years as required, in the Engineers' Shops at Taunton and any of these requiring painting etc. are in future to be sent a few at a time to Taunton addressed to Inspector Tomes for that purpose.

The arrangements for sending same must be made through Chief Inspector Shattock to whom application must be made.

The articles are to be dealt with only during the months of October, November, December, January, February and March in each year.

When being sent the name of the sending Station must be entered on the label if not already painted on the seat or board.

102

W Campfield's circular No 43   8/5/03

Bishops Lydeard

Sufferance Roads and Footpaths, Sufferance Windows. Refreshment Rooms Agreement Special Rates, Authorised Credit Accounts, Receipts and Register of Guards Watches, List of Cabs and Omnibuses plying at Station, description and position of Weighing Machines.

Payment of wages receipt, & remittance of daily cash. Fire Appliances. Keys at Station. Inventory of all non-consumable Stores etc. etc. & any other information which may be useful or desirable to record so that in the event of a change the outgoing Stationmaster shall hand over this book as containing a complete record of all special matters affecting the working of this Station.

Before recording any other matter than this book now contains, the particulars must be submitted to me that I may approve or otherwise and have the register in my Office corrected accordingly.

Petty cash allowed £5

Signed M Campfield
Superintendent
December 10th '89

Particulars of Special Instructions

Particulars	Date	By whom issued	Remarks
	24.5.86	*W Campfield*	*7/14383*

In the event of a serious accident,
and it is necessary to bring in the
breakdown gang to assist, a
telegram detailing the exact
circumstances must be
sent to Loco. Dept., Taunton

Register of Authorised Credit Accounts

Name	address	Date opened	length of credit to be given	reference to Authority
Ms Baines	Bishops Lydeard	4.5.87	month	Supt. 1/1330
Ms Esdaite	" "	7.3.88	"	Supt. 1/1330
Ms Aylesbury	" "	7.3.88	"	Supt. 1/1330
Major Belfield	Bagboro'	Aug. 28th 1908	"	Supt. 1/1330

Agreements, Sufferance Roads, Windows passes etc. etc.

Particulars	date	by whom issued	Reference
Agreement for the preservation of game on the slopes of the Railway	13.5.87	General Manager Agreement No 8105	9.3287

Mr S F Bissett	Lessee
John Barker	}
Edwin "	} Gamekeepers
Wm "	}

Permits available between
170¾ & 171¾ mile posts
£1 a year.

Passenger trains must not be backed into the Goodshed Siding either to take on or to shunt off Horseboxes or other vehicles, but in all cases the vehicles must be pushed out of or into the Siding as the case may be.

W. Campfield N 4/10452 16//11/93

Passenger Trains may now be backed into the Goodshed Siding either to take on or shunt off Horseboxes or other vehicles.

W. O Morris W2/28990 Oct. 1896

List of Offices and other Keys at Station and where kept:

Offices	No	Where kept and to be found during the day	Night
Yard Gate	1	Stationmaster's possession	Cabin
Goods Shed	1	"	"
Cabin	1	"	Office
Office Front Door	1	"	"
Side Entrance duty	1	"	Porter on early
Waiting Room	2	"	Office
Lamp Room	1	"	"
Coalhouse	1	"	"
Petroleum Lockup	1	"	"

Inventory of Furniture and Non-consumable Stores at Station

Where kept or placed	No.	Description of article	Date supplied	Remarks
Waiting Room	1	Benches, stuffed	1861	
" "	6	Chairs	"	Wooden bottom
" "	1	Coal Scuttle	"	
" "	1	Fender	"	
" "	1 set	Fire Irons	"	
" "	1	Looking glass	"	
" "	1	Table (oak)	"	
" "	2	Towels	"	
" "	1	Wash hand stand	"	
Booking Office	2	Blinds	"	

"	"	2	Blinds Roller	"
"	"	2	Cash Bags	"
"	"	3	Cash Bowels (sic)	"
"	"	2	Chairs, wood	"
"	"	1	Date boxes	"
"	"	2	Desk, sloped	"
"	"	1	Fenders	"
"	"	3	Ink stands, glass	"
"	"	2	Ink stands, metal	"
"	"	1	Letter Press, invoice size	"
"	"	1	Paper Cases, tin	"
"	"	1	Rulers	"
"	"	1	Stools, leather seated	"
"	"	1	Tables, deal	"
"	"	2	Telegraph batteries	1861
"	"	1	Telegraph Instruments	"
"	"	1	Tickets case, issuing	"
"	"	1	Ticket Dating Presses	"
"	"	1	Twine box	"
"	"	1	Cash Safe	Oct. 1889
Parcels Office		1	Label Case	1861
"	"	1	Paste pot	"
"	"	1	Brushes, house	"
Lobby		1	Clock	"
"		1	Weighing machine	"
"		1	Passenger fare list & frame	"
"		1	Silver Lamp	1886
Booking Office		1	" "	"
Waiting Room		1	" "	1887
Signal Cabin		1	" " , swing	1884
"	"	1	Telegraph batteries	1861

"	"	1	Telegraph Instruments	"	
"	"	1	Coal Scuttle	1887	
"	"	1	Form	"	
"	"	1	Hatchet	"	
"	"	1	Fender	"	
"	"	2	Fire Irons	"	
"	"	1	Nippers, cancelling	"	
"	"	1	Nippers, round hole	"	
Lamp Room		9	Signal lamps	no record	
"	"	3	Guard Lamps	"	
"	"	3	Oil tins	1861	
"	"	1	Oil feeder	"	
"	"	1	Oil funnel tin	"	
"	"	5	Platform lamps	"	
"	"	11	" "	1917	
Platform		2	Stools, wooden	1861	
"		1	Pair sack trucks	"	
"		1	Wheel barrow	"	
"		5	Platform lamp cases	"	
"		11	" " "		
			with station name		
"		1	4 wheel trolley	1889	
"		1	" "	1907	
Yard		1	Towing rope	1887	
"		1	Lever, Iron shod	1861	
Coal House		1	Shovel	"	
Lamp Room		2	Baskets to (?) cases	"	
Goods Shed		1	Hook and chain, dog	"	
"	"	1	Hook and chain, wool	"	
"	"	1	Van board	"	
"	"	1	Weighing machine	"	
"	"	1	Padlock (switch)	"	on door

Yard Gates	2	Padlock (switch)	"	on gates
Cattle pens	2	Padlock (switch)	"	" "
" "	1	Lamp case	1907	
In Yard	1	Oil House tin	1883	
Office	3	Towels	"	
"	3	Dusters	"	
Signal Cabin	1	Towel	1883	
Office	2	Desks	"	
Urinal	1	Buckets, iron	"	
"	1	Bass Broom	"	
Passenger platform	2	Sheets for platform trolleys	Jan 16th 1914	

Author's note

I had been unable to ascertain exactly when the sidings at Bishops Lydeard were laid out. On a map of 1880 they were not shown, but they appeared on a map dated 1892. It was only when I studied the above inventory and saw the items that had been obtained in 1882/3, that I realised I had found the answer to the problem that had been puzzling me.

Special rates for the conveyance of Market and perishable traffic by passenger Train

Station to	Description of traffic	Rates per cwt			Date of service	Route
		Or	Cr	Min		
Birmingham	Live poultry & eggs			1 cwt		GWR/MID
Birmingham	Dead poultry game meat rabbit			½ cwt		GWR/MID
Bristol	Fish & ice	2s 0d	2s 8d	½ cwt	10/4/83	GWR/MID
Didsbury	Harrisons hprs (sic)	half	full	1s 0d	10/4/83	GWR/MID
Plymouth	Ice	2s 6d	3s 4d	1 cwt	28/6/83	
Bristol	Hearnes hprs	half	full	6d only	7/8/85	GWR
Manchester	Dead rabbits & game	5s 0d	6s 8d	½ cwt	16/9/90	GWR/LY
Lincoln	Do	5s 3d	7s 0d	Do	16/9/90	GWR/LNWR
Leeds	Do	5s 6d	7s 4d	Do	16/9/90	GWR/LNWR
Bradford	Do	5s 6d	7s 4d	Do	16/9/90	Do
Leicester	Do	4s 6d	6s 0d	Do	16/9/90	Do
Bristol	Bakers' tray, veg			1s 0d	19/8/91	GWR
Birmingham	Live poultry & eggs	4s 0d	full	1 cwt	27/10/91	GWR/MID
Birmingham	Dead poultry meat and rabbits	3s 9d	5s 0d	½ cwt	27/10/91	GWR/MID
Bristol	Watercress	2s 0d	2s 8d	Do	21/11/91	GWR
Birmingham	Mushrooms	3s 9d	5s 0d	Do	31/8/98	GWR/MID
Sheffield	do	5s 0d	6s 8d	Do	17/9/98	GWR/LY
Manchester	do	5s 0d	6s 8d	Do	do	Do
Bradford (Yorks)	do	5s 6d	7s 4d	Do	do	Do
Halifax	Game poultry rabbits, dead	5s 0d		1 cwt	11/1/04	Do

Poster Boards GWR

	single	double	broad side
In Up waiting room	2	1	1
In Down waiting room	1		1
On Down platform	5	2	1
On signalman's landing	1		
Total	9	3	3
Miscellaneous	11		
Pictorial	1		
Excursion	2		3
LSWR On Down platform			1
Midland Railway on Down platform	1		
London & North Western Railway on Down platform			1

Other information included in this log book included the serial numbers of receipt books issued, the last entry in this section being in 1925. Also included were the dates on which the various weighing machines around the station were checked or sent away for repair, and the latest entry in this section is in 1932. Similar records are included for the testing, return for repair or replacement, of crane chains and ropes, also 'Dog' and 'Wool' hooks, the last entry in this section being in 1929.

Perhaps the most fascinating entries in this section relate to the various time-pieces that were sent away for repair. One particular time-piece that appeared to spend more time away being repaired than it was in service, was number 4108. Its history is as follows:

		Remarks:
Sent for repair 22/5/23	Returned repaired 17/7/23	Ring missing on return
Sent for repair 13/9/24	Returned repaired 5/11/24	Repaired Swindon
Sent for repair 31/8/26	Returned repaired 8/10/26	Repaired Exeter
Sent for repair 19/8/27	Returned repaired 8/9/27	Repaired Exeter
Sent for repair 3/10/27	Returned repaired 30/11/27	Repaired Exeter
Sent for repair 24/8/28	Returned repaired 30/10/28	Repaired Exeter
Sent for repair 1/4/29	Returned repaired 18/6/29	Repaired Exeter
Sent for repair 30/10/29	Returned repaired 17/12/31	??

After the long time spent away for repair at an unrecorded location, there are no further recorded entries for this luckless time-piece: were its problems finally corrected? Or did the luckless user decide that it would be better if he purchased his own time-piece? Did it continue to give problems and were they recorded in a later logbook?

It is interesting to note that the first dated entry in the book is in 1883, although it would appear that some undated entries were recorded before this date. Therefore the log was in general use at the station for a period of roughly fifty years. It is hard to believe that any equipment in use these days would remain in service for such a prolonged period and at the same time provide such an insight into the lives and the characters who used it.